One Pan Gourmet

Fresh Food on the Trail

Second Edition

Don Jacobson

Ragged Mountain Press/McGraw-Hill
Camden, Maine • New York • Chicago • San Francisco •
Lisbon • London • Madrid • Mexico City • Milan • New Delhi •
San Juan • Seoul • Singapore • Sydney • Toronto

The McGraw·Hill Companies

1 2 3 4 5 6 7 8 9 10 DOC DOC 0 9 8 7 6 5

Library of Congress Cataloging-in-Publication Data
Jacobson, Donald.
The one pan gourmet : fresh food on the trail / Don Jacobson.—2nd ed.
        p.   cm.
Includes index.
ISBN 0-07-144317-7 (pbk. : alk. paper)
1. Outdoor cookery. 2. One-dish meals. 3. Camping—Equipment and supplies. I. Title.
TX823.J34 2005
641.5′78—dc22   2004027384

Questions regarding the content of this book should be addressed to
Ragged Mountain Press
P.O. Box 220
Camden, ME 04843
www.raggedmountainpress.com

Questions regarding the ordering of this book should be addressed to
The McGraw-Hill Companies
Customer Service Department
P.O. Box 547
Blacklick, OH 43004
Retail customers: 1-800-262-4729
Bookstores: 1-800-722-4726

Photos by the author unless otherwise noted.

CONTENTS

ACKNOWLEDGMENTS AND NOTES TO THE SECOND EDITION

Just as in many endeavors, there's probably nothing in cooking that hasn't been tried a thousand times before. I have to tip my culinary hat to all those enterprising cooks who, over the years, have tried to brighten the insides of their friends, families, and neighbors.

The reader, especially an experienced cook, will find that many of the recipes are old favorites presented with a slight twist. And that's the intent of this little work—to give a new look to campsite and trail cooking.

Many people have contributed to the recipes in this book, usually by testing them. The young men of Boy Scout Troop 80 in Downers Grove, Illinois, and the members of the Old Turkey patrol, especially dedicated Wood Badge Scouter Jim Baldwin, have been most eager and gracious in this respect. Other folks, such as Toby Erickson, an interpreter at the Charles L. Sommers National High Adventure Base (Boy Scouts of America), showed me that there are many who love to eat in the outdoors.

The lion's share of my gratitude, however, goes to three people who have encouraged my cooking efforts more than any others: to my father and mother, who taught me how to take the offerings provided by a teacher's pay and turn them into daily feasts; and to my wife and partner, Pam, whose comments have helped keep me honest and who always urges me to create new recipes for our table. Pam, a registered dietitian, has been a huge contributor to this process. As I write this, she is completing her master's degree in nutrition at Northern Illinois University. Her insights, information, and exposure to the science that is behind everything we eat have profoundly educated me. To her goes a boundless measure of thanks and love.

I would also like to express my thanks to the product specialists at REI's corporate headquarters in Seattle. I have been a co-op member since 1966, and I've always known why. Their support is a reminder that more goes into outdoor cooking gear than just price and packaging. Thanks also to Ann Walden of The Coleman Company and to the team at GSI Outdoors for their help in putting the latest information in my hands.

It is all those hikers and campers on the trails of New Hampshire, Illinois, and California who deserve the final credit. These hardy folks give me continued pleasure when I meet and learn from them among the trees and mountains of our country's wilderness.

In the end, my largest thanks is to all my trekking cohorts, whether you tie on hiking boots, hop on a touring bike, or step into a canoe or kayak. This book is for you, if you've ever made camp with nothing more inspiring than the prospect of a can of beans or a hot dog to dull the edge on your appetite. My hope is to make your experience a bit better, your trip a mite more enjoyable, your meals more fun. Here's a wave of the spoon to you!

As written, the recipes in this book serve two average persons average portions, or one person quite generously. If you are cooking for yourself, you can adjust most of the recipes simply by halving the main ingredients and cutting back somewhat on the spices. The same logic, but in reverse, applies when cooking for more than two (or for two very hungry people!). In general, increase the amounts by 50 percent for three people. For four, double everything. You can also always bump up the vegetables, sauces, and side dishes to fill the empty spaces.

The cookware recommended in The Portable Kitchen chapter will feed one or two, but for bigger groups you'll want a larger (10- to 12-inch) frying pan and a two-quart pot. And the oven alone will not suffice for a big crowd; you could cook the meat portions in it, but you won't have room for the vegetables. On the other hand, more people mean more backpacks to carry cookware, so it all works out.

Finally, writing this book has taught me what personal expressions cooking and eating are. My biases and preferences are reflected throughout—it could be no other way. For example, I am fussy enough about cooking oils to carry small portions of four kinds (vegetable, olive, peanut, and corn) into the wilderness when my weekend menu calls for them. And I'm an omnivore. I like meat as much as vegetables, and my meals usually include both. Still, thanks to Chris Townsend and others, there are many delicious vegetarian recipes here; the Oven chapter has a section called Vegetarian Delights (see pages 141–47), but other chapters have meatless dishes as well. Or you can adapt many recipes by simply leaving out the meat. The index will help you find anything you're looking for. The meat substitution ideas and the protein complementation chart (pages 27–28) reinforce the fact that outdoor adventures and vegetarianism are *not* incompatible. In fact, they can fit together quite nicely.

The world has changed considerably since *The One Pan Gourmet* took its first bow in 1993. One could argue the merits of where we have come in the past dozen years, but I'll not do that here. However, I have changed my approach to food to an extent. I watch saturated fat and overall calories, and—for those who feel likewise—I've supplied appropriate substitution suggestions in the recipes in this edition. And I've added recipes that reflect new cooking interests of mine.

Read on, and eat well!

INTRODUCTION

No one has ever accused me of missing a meal intention-
ally. In fact, sometimes my girth has gotten in the way of
friendships, relationships, even the sun on the beach.

Oh, I'm not obese or even pleasingly plump. There's just
some extra padding on my frame that could—should—be
taken off for health's sake.

And that's one reason I camp, hike, take day outings,
and generally sweat, grunt, and groan my way up the
White Mountains, across the Angeles Crest, and back
down the Berkshires. And it's why I canoe the Boundary
Waters. More recently, I jump on my Fuji TI and put 20,
63, 100, or even 500 miles under my wheels. I simply can't
think of a better way to work off unwanted lard than by
burning it up in the company of good friends and Mother
Nature.

Funny thing is, the more you walk, paddle, or pedal, the
more calories you burn and the hungrier you get. The hungrier you are, the more you want to eat. And that, as the
Bard put it, is the rub.

Hiking, biking, canoeing, kayaking, and camping are
emotional as well as physical experiences that should
leave the soul as refreshed as the body is exhausted. As I
have clambered around this nation's backroads, hills, and
mountains, I have learned that the visual and tactile plea-
sures of hiking—grand though they be—are not the total-
ity of the outdoor experience.

Think about this for a moment: On the trail, you wake
up about 6:30 or 7:00 in the morning. You eat. You pack
your gear and start walking.

Along the way, you see towering crags, sweeping vistas, hawks, songbirds, alpine lakes . . . and the cares of your workaday world fade into the recesses of your mind, and eventually out of it altogether.

Then you stop to eat.

Back on the trail at 1:00, you point out the mountain laurel or piñon pines, talk about the condition of the trail and your feet, and start looking closely at the distance you have to cover before setting up camp that night. Why? Because you want to be sure you'll have enough daylight left to cook dinner.

Getting to the site, you pitch your tent, roll out your sleeping bag, break out your cooking gear and food, and concoct dinner.

Then you eat.

Maybe before turning in after an evening's storytelling, you have a snack or a drink. Have you picked up a consistent theme here?

On the average backpacking trip, hiker-campers really do three basic things: They sleep. They hike. They eat. And paddlers and pedalers are no different.

With rest breaks included, the most you can spend on the trail without absolutely killing yourself is about nine hours or so. If you average an hour or two for making and breaking camp, and a generous ten hours of sleep, that still leaves about four hours for cooking, eating, and related activities.

Nearly 30 percent of your waking hours spent in camp are often occupied with considering how to replace the calories you have worked off.

So don't tell me you want to kick back, boil some water, and feast on a freeze-dried brick called Chicken Gumbo so you can save preparation time.

Consider the alternative—something fresh, with crisp vegetables, a succulent sauce, and that toothsome, satisfying, filling feeling only real food can give. Perhaps a nice dessert. Something to be savored, not tolerated. Something that encourages companions to linger over the evening meal and the ensuing conversation. Something that soothes the digestion, improves your outlook, chases away the gloom of an unwelcome rainstorm, and requires a whole lot less water to prepare than the freeze-dried alternatives.

The simple fact is that all too many trekkers have been brainwashed into thinking that, along with their high-tech sleeping bag, tent, stove, boots, and other gear, they have to spend immense amounts of money for high-tech food in order to save weight. Unless your trips are measured in weeks rather than days, it simply isn't so.

The human race managed nicely for more than 5,000 years of recorded history without freeze-dried foods. (I do bow to parched corn and beans, however.) Hannibal crossed the Alps without beef stew in a bag. Lindbergh crossed the Atlantic with a couple of ham sandwiches.

So take charge of your stomach. You, too, can eat the way you like in the outdoors. Grab your frying pan, your pot, or your oven, and live the one-pan lifestyle!

A PHILOSOPHY OF EATING

It seems there are only two schools of thought when it comes to eating in the backcountry. Either you're cooking out of the trunk of your car on a multiburner stove stoked by a huge tank of propane, or you're a minimalist subsisting on dried fruit and freeze-dried pouch food. In the first case you're not really in the backcountry, and in the second case, in my opinion, you're not really eating.

I'll not take issue with my comrades of the high ranges and wild rivers who depend so heavily on freeze-dried foods. To cut their supply line for weeks at a time, they must compromise between comfort and convenience. So they pack a bunch of expensive foil packs, rice, pasta, beans, a water filter, and extra rolls of toilet paper.

I don't camp out of my car except on rare occasions. That eliminates the 12-gallon cooler and crown roasts of lamb. Yet I reject the premise that you have to become an ascetic to enjoy the aesthetics of the great outdoors. Since I don't often spend more than two nights on the trail, I don't need to worry about gear weight as much as the long-haul hikers and wilderness trippers do. And I sure don't need to drop five bucks a meal for something that, when ready, does not resemble food.

DIET AT HOME . . . EAT ON THE TRAIL

You need calories when you are on the trail. No matter how fit you are or how much you weigh, you are going to burn a few thousand calories to power the engine that drives you up hill and down dale. It doesn't make sense to skimp when it comes to eating, which means you should eat "three squares" plus snacks to stoke the fires between meals. A decent breakfast will get you moving faster than any dash of ice water and will keep you going longer. Lunch can be a little lighter if you want, but try to hit all the basic food groups—including grains, protein, vegetables, and fruits. Fruit is important: apples, pears, and peaches are Mother Nature's no-need-to-cook, ready-to-eat convenience foods. Stuff one or two in a side pocket in your pack. Grab and munch anytime. They're biodegradable and leave no nasty plastic wrappers to carry out.

Then there's dinner. The end of the day. The pinnacle of the hiking experience. Again, balance and variety should be the watchwords.

I've been hiking since I was a kid. And I've learned that, although you can get calories from almost anything, it's much more fun if you take the time to plan genuinely good meals. The happiest campers I've seen are the ones with full bellies. It doesn't matter if those stomachs are hidden inside hyperactive 11-year-olds or weighing down normally office-bound boomers, Xers, or Yers. Fill them up and there are smiles. Let the needle hit empty and the growls will drown out even the mosquitoes. Fill their bellies with delicious fresh food and the planets will align and the music of the heavenly spheres will become audible.

I believe the time you spend in camp can and should be just as rewarding as the time spent walking. And a major part of that time ought to involve food preparation. As far as I'm concerned, it's not drudgery to add freshly sliced veggies to a broth simmering around a couple of succulent chops. In fact, I savor those moments as much as a scenic vista graced by the widespread wings of a single peregrine.

You need not be bent over the stove continuously for two or three hours. Good food should be left to itself, to blend its flavors and work its magic in secret. With the prep work out of the way and the food in the pot, pan, or oven, take a few minutes to organize yourself for dinner. Clean up. Read. Tighten the tent ropes. Darn a sock. Grab a camera and shoot the sights around you.

Then you can eat the way the French do—taking your time, digging into something that is really worth enjoying, and appreciating the fact that you cooked it. What you are doing, of course, is paying yourself the ultimate compliment: that you do deserve to live well.

A QUESTION OF BALANCE: HARDWARE OR MUNCHWARE?

Even for the weekend backpacker, enjoyment varies inversely with the weight of the pack. The heavier your sack, the less fun you'll have.

One of the reasons your pack may be too heavy is that you are trying to bring all the comforts of home when you should be thinking about blending into the scenery as much as possible. I'm talking about low-impact camping.

Low-impact camping is a philosophy best embodied in the catch phrase, "Take nothing but pictures, leave nothing but footprints." It's that simple. People should not be outsiders when outdoors. They should become part of the picture, deemphasizing their individuality and perceived importance in the face of Creation's grandeur.

Entire books are devoted to this subject. For my money, *The National Outdoor Leadership School's Wilderness Guide* (www.nols.edu) offers the best discussion about all aspects of living outdoors. After you've done it for a few years, loading up your backpack and eliminating excess fripperies and weight becomes a habit, not a conscious thought process.

You simply cannot do without certain things when it comes to camping. Most of what you have to take along involves housing—tent, ground cloth, rainfly, tent stakes, and mallet. (Shelter is particularly important in the wet and buggy East. Eastern campers are always amazed the first time they sleep under the stars in the West and are not tormented by mosquitoes all night.) Of course, you'll also need your sleeping bag, sleeping pad, and, if you remember, pillow.

Add your survival and first-aid gear, spare clothes, bug repellent, toilet paper, extra line, and water, and you've got the makings of a load. To cover my own needs, I carry at least 3 quarts of water in my pack. No, not a quart per day. I fill up my bottles before I leave home. With a little luck, the water will last through to the next evening. Then I grab my water filter and refill all the bottles.

How about a deck of cards, a book, a camera? We've already got a lot in our pack, but not one bit of food. Where are we going to find room?

Simple question: Which is more important? Food or metal?

Food? Good, you can walk on my trail anytime.

If you have limited space but don't want to sacrifice the amount or type of food, you have only two items to cut— the stove (sure) or the cookware.

Over time I've learned that you never use every pot you carry. So I've eliminated most of the hardware provided in cook kits from my pack. I keep the cup, and I have a little teapot for boiling coffee water. But a frying pan . . . and a small pot . . . and a big pot are redundant.

We're not saving a lot of weight here, maybe a pound on the outside. But we are saving space. A frying pan tucks into the corner of the pack behind a tent or under some socks. A pot nestles on top of a stove or holds more clothes. And if you bring only one pan or pot, you'll save valuable space. And you'll challenge yourself to create interesting menus that take full advantage of that one pan.

And isn't that what trekking is all about? Taking the challenge to walk that extra mile? To climb that higher mountain? To impress yourself, your family and friends with your culinary skills on the trail?

I have been cooking out of one pan for years. Usually, the smells and tastes are just for me alone, but every once in a while I share my efforts with somebody else who ends up bringing something different to the party. Maybe it's a new recipe for chili. Maybe it's a hot drink I've never tried.

This sharing of hospitality is traditional on the trail, as fitting as a cowboy offering a cup of coffee to a stranger coming in out of the howling wastes. Food builds a bond, if only for a few hours, between people sharing a common, though uniquely separate, experience.

I've never had a problem building something that feeds two out of only one frying pan or stew pot. And usually that something brings a smile and, once in a while, a hand or two of gin rummy.

Even if you never simplify your camping kitchen to include just one pan, the fostering in your heart of the emotion that exemplifies one-pan hospitality will warm your spirit more than the finest Bordeaux.

THE PORTABLE KITCHEN

If you're planning to be a wilderness chef, you'll need a kitchen that lets you pursue culinary quests without enormous effort. With green trees or a rich blue sky as a canopy, you should be enjoying the aromas and tastes of your creations, not cursing a cracked cutting board or missing measuring spoons. Remember, good cooking can't be done without the right equipment.

As suggested in the last chapter, the fewer pieces of kitchen hardware you carry, the better. Give me a tablespoon measure, a Sierra cup (see photo on page 8), the palm of my hand, a sharp knife, and a cutting board and I'll be happy as a pig in a corn crib. Of course, there are times when a few extra goodies make a pleasant difference. But let's stick to basics. They'll do the job, and they're lighter, too.

UTILITARIAN UTENSILS

Once upon a time, the state of the art in camping gear was stainless steel. Steel didn't rust, it lasted forever . . . and it weighed a ton. For my first Christmas as a Boy Scout I got everything, including a stainless Scout fork, knife, and spoon set. The plastic carrying case has long since melted in some forgotten fire, but the three pieces of heavy metal are still slicing bacon, spearing chicken chunks, and stirring coffee. Stainless steel utensils remain a reasonable choice.

But now I have just one word for you—Lexan. Utensils made of Lexan, a polycarbonate material, are incredibly durable (though not flame- or heatproof) and light weight. And Lexan utensils are gentle on anodized pots and pans. Other plastics—such as bottles, vials, and tubes to carry spices, condiments, and oils—have also lightened the camper's load.

I have been using a Camper Kitchen Kit, manufactured by Outdoor Research (www.orgear.com), to keep my kitchen tools and other items together. It crams everything you need into a compact carrying case: a fork-knife-spoon set, a large spoon, a spatula, measuring spoons, and a miniwhisk—as well as a spice rack of salt and pepper, oils, grated cheese, and any number of liquids and powders. Everything is in one easy-to-find case rather than scattered around various pockets in your pack. Customize your own kitchen with OR's Kitchen Pouch and as many vials and spoons (and so forth) as you want.

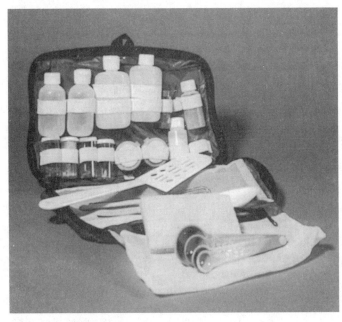

The outdoor kitchen.

Still life: Sierra cup, cutting board, potgrabs, water bottle,
utensils.

   Add to this a nonporous cutting board, hot-pot tongs
(potgrabs), pot holder, plate, Sierra cup or equivalent (for
coffee, oatmeal, scooping servings out of a pot, etc.), and
carving knife, and you have a basic field kitchen.

   Of course, you don't have to buy a special (and poten-
tially expensive) outfit. All you have to do is assemble the
equipment with which you feel most comfortable. I've
provided a sample checklist opposite.

   Most of the items can be packed in a few drawstring
bags. Put the stove (more about that later), fuel funnel (if
using white gas or kerosene), and hot-pot tongs in one
bag. Your fuel bottle or spare canisters can go in an easy-
to-reach outside pack pocket. And don't forget the
matches, even if your stove has a Piezo electric igniter.
These are somewhat fragile and they do break. In that
case, a match may be the difference between raw rice and
teriyaki. I know because I light my stove using Diamond
Match Blues. In fact, it's a good idea to bring several packs
or boxes of waterproof matches and scatter them throughout your pack and clothing.

FIELD KITCHEN CHECKLIST

Personal Gear

fork, knife, spoon	plate or bowl
metal cup	water bottle

Kitchen Hardware

hot-pot tongs or potgrabs	nested teaspoon/tablespoon
pot holder	measures
cutting board	large knife
coffee-/teapot	aluminum foil
frying pan or pot (pick one)	miniwhisk
backpacking stove	backpacking oven (optional)
extra fuel in sealed	trash bag
container	3 or 4 metal tent stakes
funnel for fuel (if needed)	liquid soap
waterproof matches	steel wool scrub pad
spatula	

Kitchen Software (depending on recipes selected)

salt	marjoram
seasoned salt	bay leaves
pepper	paprika
onion flakes	oregano
garlic powder	other spices
celery salt	grated Parmesan cheese
hot sauce	instant or real coffee
Cajun spices	tea bags
basil	bouillon cubes
thyme	sugar

vegetable, olive, peanut, and/or corn oils (pack as needed for recipes selected) and/or nonstick cooking spray

Waterproofing matches is something every Scout knows how to do. For those of you who missed this fun recreational activity, here's how you do it: In a double boiler (if you don't own one, float a 1-pint saucepan in a 1-quart pot about half full of water), melt some paraffin. **Never melt the wax over direct heat. It could flame suddenly, causing serious burns.** Bundle about 10 wooden kitchen matches with heavy thread and, holding the tail of the thread, dip the heads and about an inch of the matches into the wax. Remove and let cool to harden. Voilà, waterproof matches!

Put the rest of your gear into other bags or pack pockets as you deem appropriate. I like to keep it all together in one easy-to-find place. There's nothing worse than your piping-hot coffee turning to lukewarm mud while you rustle through the pack looking for the sugar.

Kitchens, like computers, need "software" to function well. And in the kitchen, your software consists of season-ings, spices, and oils. It's most efficient to pack only what you need for each trip in small plastic vials or other unbreakable containers. An excellent alternative is a seven-day pill box; label each compartment with white adhesive tape. Another possibility is the plastic canisters used to store 35 mm film, although these little treasures are becoming more difficult to find as digital photography becomes increasingly popular. (Make friends with your local express photo-processing lab; if anybody has them, these folks will.) Whatever you do, make sure you label your spices clearly. No sense in trying to guess which is thyme and which is marjoram.

Note that I try to recommend oils for seasoning pur-poses only. I pack them in 4-ounce bottles. To keep food from sticking to pans (and to avoid adding fat and calories), try using a nonstick cooking spray like Pam or Vegalene.

A FEW THOUGHTS ABOUT WATER

Trekkers have to contend with water availability wherever they travel, and water quality is of even greater concern. One way around the issue is to carry all your water, but you need several quarts per person per day just to avoid dehydration. Since water weighs about 8 pounds per gal-lon, the equation is certainly not in your favor even on short trips. There's no way around relying on local sources to keep your water bottles full.

And that means purifying the water you plan to drink or use in cooking in order to kill off bacteria and other nasty critters. That's easily accomplished by adding chlorine tablets or iodine crystals, tablets, or liquid (which most experts agree to be superior to chlorination), or by boiling the water for 5 to 10 minutes. You can filter out silt and solid matter by pouring the water through a handkerchief or other cloth strainer before purification.

Iodine or chlorine treatment, however, imparts an unpleasant taste to the water (commonly counteracted with Kool-Aid or some such powdered drink mix), and boiling is often impractical because it takes time and fuel. On top of that, chemical purification alone does not combat the nasty protozoan cyst named *Giardia lamblia*. *Giardia* is a hard-shelled microorganism that *usually* succumbs to boiling and chlorine or iodine purification methods. It lives in your lower gastrointestinal tract and does its best to make your life miserable for many, many months. You won't know if the water you're using is infested for seven to ten days, so "usually" is not good enough in my book.

Likewise, another cyst, *Cryptosporidium parvum*, has been found to infest fecal-tainted backcountry waters. *Crypto* is pretty much impervious to chemical treatment. Symptoms of cryptosporidiosis appear in two to ten days and last, thankfully, for about two weeks. I say "thankfully" because unlike giardiasis, crypto cannot be treated with a prescription.

The best way to deal with *Giardia* and *Crypto* is to use a water filtration or purification system. The essential difference between a filtration system and a purification system is that a filtration unit removes bacteria and cysts from raw water. A purifier does that and, using either an iodine resin or electrostatic charge, eliminates viruses that are smaller than the 0.2 micron openings in most ceramic filter elements. There are several on the market, with prices ranging up to about $100. All enable you to take water directly from almost any source and remove *Giardia*,

Crypto, bacteria, and other objectionable things. According to REI, a leading outdoor equipment manufacturer and retailer, some of the most important features to consider are removable filters, quality of pump manufacture, output, and speed of filtration.

Remember to look at the filter porosity size, and make sure it is 0.2 micron. *Giardia* cysts range between 5 and 15 microns. *Crypto* cysts are smaller, between 2 and 5 microns. Using a filter with a 0.2 micron pore size will ensure that you get most of the bad out.

There is one exception to the absolute need to filter for *Giardia*. If you're canoeing or boating in a lake and can get more than 100 feet offshore into water that is 20 feet deep or more, you can dip your pot with a greater degree of confidence. The reason is that *Giardia* has a hard shell and is relatively heavy for its size, so it sinks to the bottom. This means that the traditionally accepted place for good water—a bubbling stream or at the base of a crystalline waterfall—is a big no-no unless you are carrying a decent filtration-purification system. The bottom is constantly being roiled, keeping *Giardia* and *Crypto* in circulation.

If you'd like to learn more about water purification and filtration techniques and equipment, I suggest you visit www.rei.com and click on the Expert Advice icon. You'll find an incredible amount of information about water and the backpacker.

PROMETHEUS, THE CAMPER

The key to good camp cooking is an excellent heat source.

Ancient Greeks and Romans, as well as more contemporary Pilgrims and Conestoga settlers, enjoyed a bountiful supply of wood and a low ecological consciousness. A roaring fire was part of every campsite. Seared meat, either over- or undercooked breads, and enough soot and ash to make any Gothamite proud were the rule.

But consider these facts before pulling out your ax or saw.

Keeping it clean: MSR MiniWorks EX water filter. *Courtesy REI.*

- An open fire is not a particularly efficient way to cook anything short of a steer on a spit. Even then, you had better like your meat blood-red rare or shoe-leather well done.
- Backpackers can't afford to participate in denuding our forests or adding the impact of an open fire to an environment already stressed to the maximum. Smoke and soot from your fire just heap insult upon the injury caused by factories and cars hundreds of miles to the west of that forest or just upstream from that beautiful gorge. And the next hikers to pass that way won't enjoy the sight of your fire ring any more than they would the sight of a beer can or a strand of pink toilet paper in the forest litter.
- The Forest Service has better things to do than put out wildfires caused by careless campers.

Since the late 1950s compact backpacking stoves pioneered by the mountain-climbing fraternity have been available through many high-quality outfitters. Over the years the fuels of choice have varied from kerosene to white gas, isobutane mix, butane, or propane. All have advantages and disadvantages.

Kerosene (diesel fuel) is readily available around the world, so if you're planning to travel overseas, a kerosene-burning stove might be the answer. Kerosene is difficult to light, however, and the quality of the fuel can vary from location to location. Pack a strainer—seriously—to remove the larger particles of debris from the distillate. Otherwise you'll clog the jets in your stove instantly, putting you and your comrades on a forced diet.

The most popular fuel for one-burner backpacking stoves is white gas—Coleman fuel. Available in camping supply stores, convenience marts, and gas stations, white gas ignites readily in cold or hot weather, providing optimum heat production. White gas is easily found in the United States, but is hard to locate elsewhere.

Alcohol stoves are more popular in Europe than North America. I haven't used one, so I can't comment on their cooking qualities. But alcohol is less volatile than white gas and burns cooler, so you will likely want to cook your meals a bit longer than the recipes suggest.

Propane and butane ignite readily and provide instant heat. You cannot spill fuel but that is because it is packaged in a metal cartridge that adds weight and must be carried back out of the wilderness. Another shortcoming is that butane will not work below 32°F. Propane will take you down to 0°.

Note that if you are traveling by air, you should plan to buy fuel at your destination.

Being an avid outdoor cook, I own a number of back-packing stoves, reflecting my history of cooking. My first, dating from the late '60s, was a Bleuet butane stove. Fueled by Gaz cartridges, this item let me cook without totally destroying my food. The cartridges lasted about an hour and weighed about 6 ounces each.

Then I got an Optimus white-gas wonder. This little

blowtorch boils water in 7 minutes or less. Balancing a frying pan on the puny windscreen is a chore, which is why the kitchen hardware list on page 9 includes tent stakes. Simply drive the stakes into the ground or snow, place the stove between them, and settle your pot on top.

The only problem with the Optimus (and similar stoves) is that the fuel tank is not pressurized. To get the fuel flowing, you have to prime the stove by dribbling a little white gas into the well at the base of the burner stem on top of the tank. Then you open the valve and light the priming fluid. There's no big flash or anything, but it tends to get messy. I've never been able to pour fuel *only* in the well, so I always end up with some on the tank or ground. (Note that I said "ground," not "floor." In every mountaineering film, the hardy souls perched at Camp V on the shoulder of Everest, melting snow for soup, are inside their tents. They have no choice. Either they cook in the tent or they starve. Outside they'd freeze solid before they could boil a cup of water. The trade-off is that they could burn to death inside their nylon tents in the event of a stove accident. No amount of food or cup of coffee is worth making that trade. Never cook in your tent.)

One of my favorite stoves is a Coleman Peak 1. There's a pump (like the one on a Coleman lantern) to pressurize the tank; the stove is self-priming. And the burner head is wide and sturdy enough to support an 8-pound Dutch oven holding a 5-pound roast with all the spuds, onions, and carrots you want. I've done it—and fed eight adults in the process. The stove doesn't weigh much and burns white gas. Over the years, I have replaced gaskets and carburetors. You can get refurb kits from Coleman (www.coleman.com). For my money, keeping my Peak 1 going is worth it. The heat control is superior. It puts out about 7,500 BTU.

Recently, I have been putting Coleman's F1 PowerBoost through its paces (see photo on page 17). This isobutane mix powerhouse weighs almost nothing (with one fuel canister, it tips the scale at about 15 ounces). The head is tiny and features a Piezo electric igniter. And at full cry, the F1 blazes in excess of 20,000 BTU. It delivers quick cooking, no fuel spillage, and pretty good heat control.

You can also try MSR's WhisperLite series or the MSR DragonFly (www.msrcorp.com). These stoves use liquid fuel in a separate tank that doubles as a fuel bottle. This eliminates refueling spillage because it is a whole lot easier to refill the MSR bottle than it is to try to hit a tilted funnel leaning out of the side of a stove. MSR and Primus are also in the canister stove business.

POT, NOT HEAD, BANGERS

My goal when I pack is to cut the weight of the cooking gear to make room for extra-special, fresh foodstuffs. So I'm careful what pots and pans I select to execute one-pan meals.

The truth is, you have to compromise. I'm a big fan of cast-iron pans, and at home I've got a skillet that's taken me about three years to break in just right. It cooks everything from omelets to cacciatore and weighs 12 pounds, which might as well be 100 from a backpacker's perspective. When my feet hit the trail, Old Faithful gets to rest in the cupboard.

The same thing goes for my Calphalon soup kettle. When you're walking, you simply can't afford even one pan that's going to put a dent in your shoulders and a crick in your back.

I tend to think aluminum when I travel the high country. It's light, fairly durable (though it will corrode), and reasonably priced. You're not going to cry too much if the handle on your aluminum 10-inch frying pan breaks. You won't get too exercised if your 1- or 2-quart boiler springs a leak or picks up a ding or two. You'll just hie yourself off to the nearest discount store and invest another $6 to $10 for a replacement.

For cooks (outdoor or otherwise), one nice thing about aluminum is that it heats up quickly and cools off just as fast. Also, a good inexpensive aluminum frying pan

Hot stuff: Coleman F1 PowerBoost. *Courtesy The Coleman Company.*

coated with one of the new nonstick surfaces makes cleanup easier. But the most salient advantage of aluminum is its light weight. Incidentally, I just commented that you could replace your frying pan if you broke the handle. Actually, I think you should consider cutting the handle off from the get-go. When you're cooking over a single burner on less than even ground, a handle can throw everything off-balance. That's why you should pack hot-pot tongs, also known as potgrabs. They are your handle. Besides, factory-issue pot handles come loose, crack, melt, fall apart, and generally make packing your backpack a pain in the neck. They always seem to be jabbing into something—your poncho, your tent, or your spine.

Because of concerns over the possible relationship between Alzheimer's disease and aluminum, uncoated aluminum outdoor cookware has pretty much vanished in the last ten years. You can get aluminum cookware, but it will tend to corrode over time with exposure to acidic foods. Now, your choices are "limited" to stainless steel, titanium, enamelware, and coated aluminum. So, it is pretty much an open field with price and use pattern being the defining criteria.

For my money, my aluminum Hard Anodized Nonstick Cook Set from GSI Outdoors (www.gsioutdoors.com) is the perfect backpacking solution. I have the 2½-quart Kit and Double Boiler. Its durable nonstick surface will last (if you use wood or Lexan utensils) for years. The pan bot-

Frying pans and potgrabs, best friends.

toms are ridged for better heat distribution. The pot lids
are also frying pans. So, no more foil tops for me.

As for which pot to include in my one-pan kit, I've
found that the 1½-quart pot fills the bill quite nicely if I'm
cooking for myself or one other person. The frying pan
from the 2½-quart pot will feed one nicely. For two, you
may want to grab a 12-inch nonstick pan.

Actually, any 1 to 1½-quart pot or kettle will do. If you
have to, you can use a larger vessel. It doesn't weigh much
more, and when packed away, the space inside will easily
store your stove, fuel bottle, and a few other essentials.

RAMPANT AMBITION . . . A ONE-PAN OVEN

Most backpackers can live happily ever after eating from
a frying pan or a pot, but there are some who want more.
These farsighted individualists realize that a world of

Going to pot. *Courtesy GSI Outdoors.*

casseroles, pies, and other delights awaits those willing to try something a bit off the wall . . . the one-pan oven.

I own three ovens suitable for backpacking or trekking. Of these, two were purchased—one for 50 cents, the other for $40. Either the Outback Oven (www.backpackers pantry.com) or the no-longer-manufactured Mirro model does the job, whether it's a roast or rolls.

If you haven't figured it out by now, I'm a very economical person . . . ah, what the . . . I'm a cheapskate. So I've found a way to put together an oven at a good price— read darn near nothing.

An oven—whether fired by gas, wood, electricity, or cow chips—cooks by convection. No direct heat is applied to the food. Rather, the environment inside the oven is warmed sufficiently to raise the temperature of the food placed inside so that it cooks. The key is creating a current of hot air (convection) inside the oven to evenly distribute the heat throughout the cooking chamber. The second requirement is keeping the food off any surface in direct contact with the heat source.

A homemade cooking chamber is easy to construct. All you have to do is drink a lot of coffee, because that way you'll have an empty 3-pound can. You may have to visit a restaurant or commercial food broker, though. Most "three-pounders" at your grocery are 39 ounces, not 48, and a 39-ounce can may be too small.

Once you have the can, a serviceable one-pan oven is just two easy steps away.

Step 1: Drill vent holes in the side of the can at the top and bottom. Using a ¼-inch drill bit, make five or six holes around the perimeter of the can just below the top rim (the open end) and another five or six just above the bottom rim (the closed end) of the can. This allows air to enter and exit the oven as hot air rises from the bottom to the top of the oven.

Step 2: Position and drill holes in the side of the can to receive rod inserts, which create a rack inside the oven

The Outback Oven.

The one-pan oven.

to support a pot. Use the same ¼-inch bit, if you wish. Locate the two grooves that run around the can—one about a third of the way up and one about two-thirds of the way up. In each groove, position two pairs of holes opposite each other to allow you to slide a tent stake, skewer, or piece of bar stock through the can. Each pair should leave about 2½ inches of space between the rods.

That gives a broad enough base to support whatever pan you choose when cooking in the oven.

By the way, if you don't have a drill, a church-key can opener will work for the vent holes. Just make sure you don't punch a hole through the bottom of the oven. Otherwise you'll have open flames blasting into the vessel, searing your food into unrecognizable slag.

The pan used in this oven must be compact. My oven is 6 inches in diameter, and my pot, a small pint vessel from an old personal cook kit, is 5½ inches across. That allows for a ¼-inch space all the way around the pot when it's placed in the oven—sufficient for the convection currents to flow.

You don't have to use a pot. You could just wrap your food in foil and place it on the rack at either of the two levels available.

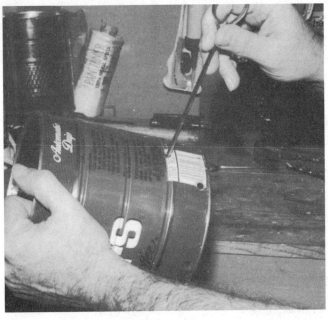

Placing rod inserts for oven base.

The two rack levels give you another way to control the cooking temperature in the oven. The lower rack position, closer to the heat source, is hotter; the upper one, cooler. You can also control the heat in the oven by raising or lowering the flame on the stove. Of course, there's no actual temperature reading here, unless you decide to bring along a meat thermometer. Trial and error is the rule with a one-pan homemade oven.

The top of the oven can be any 6-inch diameter pot lid, or foil, or anything that keeps the heat in while allowing you to get at your meal every once in a while to test it for doneness.

The oven stows away just like your pot. You can nest the stove right inside along with other cooking items. When it's time to cook, everything comes out as a unit.

PACKING IT ALL AWAY

The great thing about one-pan cooking is that there's only so much equipment available to scatter around your campsite. You don't have two frying pans, two pots, and assorted lids clanking around underfoot. That one pan or oven does its job on top of the stove, or, once cooled and cleaned, quietly nestles away in a corner of your pack awaiting its next outing.

I'm not going through the science of packing a backpack here, except to briefly summarize what works for me:

1. The left side of the inside chamber is reserved for my tent (this can strap on the outside, too), clothing, and personal items
2. The right side features all the cooking gear stacked as follows, starting from the bottom:
   - pot and oven with stove nested, or
   - stove with frying pan to one side
   - cutting board laid in vertically along the narrow side of the pack
   - kitchen kit, etc.

- fifty feet of rope and one small sack large enough to hold the food box—this is for the bear bag described on pages 38–39

3. Across the top, food stored in a Tupperware bread box
4. Water bottles are in the outside pockets or on my body

That's about all there is to it. If you think about it, most of the kitchen you'll ever need or use is based on a commonsense approach to cookery. One-panning allows you to be more flexible in your choice of accessories and menus, the subject of the next chapter.

THE FOOD

We've talked about the setup for your trail feasts. Now let's look at how to plan your fun while still in the comfort of your living room.

HOW TO PLAN A MENU

If you're an active hiker or camper, you can require upward of 2,500 calories a day during the warmer months just to keep going. In the winter, you could use up to 4,000 or more calories a day between hiking (snowshoeing) and stamping your feet. Your body is an engine powered by the food (i.e., calories) you take in. Plan any meals you like, but build plenty of high-quality calories into them. And remember that these calories must be derived from the right sources.

I'm not a vegetarian. I like a balanced diet of meat and vegetable protein. But nothing about vegetarianism is incompatible with hiking. Chris Townsend, author of *The Backpacker's Handbook*, is a vegetarian, and he's contributed a couple of his favorite recipes to this book. Chris's many 1,000-mile-plus hikes include the Continental Divide Trail from Mexico to Canada, and he's done them all without eating meat.

Whatever your preference, plan your meals to include, over the course of a day, ample quantities of the major food groups.

Dairy. Dairy products include milk, cheese, pudding, yogurt, and tofu.

Meat. Meats include lean beef, pork, poultry, fish, and shellfish; vegetarian options include dried beans, peanut butter, eggs (fresh and dehydrated), nuts, legumes, and seeds.

Vegetables and fruits. Fruits and vegetables are excellent sources of fiber (and vitamins too!). (Constipation on the trail is no more fun than it is at home—perhaps even less.) Self-packaged and easy-cooking choices include summer squash and green peppers.

Grains. Grains include cereal, noodles, pasta, rice, grits, breads, and popcorn. Stoke up on whole grains when you can.

You'll notice that most portions in this book are pretty large. At home the average size of the meat portion should be 3 to 4 ounces, but on the trail you'll need more. The suggested daily intake for a 180-pound adult male is around 2,000 to 2,200 calories, but hiking demands a lot more fuel to keep your muscles chugging along. Depending on your weight, metabolism, and the load you're carrying, you could require upward of 4,000 calories a day. Don't skimp on the food you pack. You never know when you might need an extra portion for a visitor. Or maybe that "Sunday morning out" turns into a "Sunday evening, I'm late thanks to the mud," and an extra meal will come in handy.

I've always figured an average dinner after a day of hiking, canoeing, or even bicycle touring to be about 4 to 6 ounces of meat; ¾ cup of vegetables (rehydrated if you're using dried peas, beans, etc.); about 2 to 3 ounces of bread or ½ cup of noodles or rice; and a full piece of fruit (if fresh) or ½ cup of dried fruits such as apricots, raisins, and prunes. The meat portion is elevated relative to an inactive diet
(4 to 6 ounces of lean meat per day within the context of 2,000 calories), and the carbohydrate intake is increased, yet fats are (and should be) low. Ideally, you should look at holding your fat calories to 30 percent (or less) of your daily intake. Be especially aware of the saturated fat

grams. Another 20 to 30 percent of the calories should be derived from protein. The balance (50 percent or so) is filled in by faster-burning carbs. Your needs and desires may vary. Nutritional substitutes are fine. See the following for some meat alternatives.

Meat Substitutes

To obtain the equivalent level of protein found in one ounce of meat, substitute as follows:

1 egg (although be aware of its saturated fat)
¼ cup unsalted peanuts, walnuts, almonds, pecans, or sunflower seeds
1½ cups cooked oatmeal
1 ounce cheese
2 tablespoons peanut butter
½ cup whole wheat flour

To go farther—and to ensure you get all nine amino acids essential to your body's protein synthesis—practice protein complementation. Here's how this works: The food combinations listed in the following table take advantage of protein complementation to provide a complete protein. Each item on the list contains all essential amino acids needed for protein synthesis.

FOOD COMBINATIONS

Dairy Products or Eggs with Grains

bread or rice pudding	fettucine (pasta and cheese)
cereal and milk	French toast
cheese fondue with bread	macaroni and cheese
cheese sandwich	meatless lasagna
creamed soups with noodles or rice	pancakes or waffles
eggs and toast	pizza
egg salad sandwich	quiche
	yogurt and crackers

(continued)

FOOD COMBINATIONS *(continued)*

Grains with Legumes

baked beans and brown
   bread
bean and rice dishes
bean or lentil soup and
   bread
corn tortillas or tacos and
   beans
hummus and bread
lentils and rice

peanut butter sandwich
soybean sandwich
split pea soup and
   cornbread
tamale pie (beans and
   cornmeal)
quinoa (a complete protein
   package in itself)

Nuts and Seeds with Legumes

bean soup with sesame seed
   muffins
hummus with sesame seeds
nuts and seed snacks

roasted soybeans and seed
   snacks
tofu with sesame seeds

Other Vegetables with Dairy Products or Eggs

bean-cheese salad
cream of vegetable soup
eggplant-artichoke
   parmesan
potato salad with egg

scalloped potatoes
spinach or broccoli quiche
spinach salad with eggs and
   cheese

The bottom line is this: No one-pan menu is complete unless you obtain the nourishment you need to get up and keep going. Plan smart. Eat balanced meals.

Notes on Eating "Lite"

We can all agree that taking the high trail demands a lot of calories. But, as I mentioned above, you have to make sure they come from the "right" sources. That means a good mix of carbohydrates, protein, and fat. Too much fat and you defeat your efforts to use trekking as part of a healthy lifestyle. Not enough fat or protein at the right time and you could reduce your performance and maybe even affect your health.

The "standard" American diet has, in recent years, skewed decidedly toward an overabundance of calories generated by sugars and fat. We also get stuck with the added fat that usually goes hand-in-hand with many cuts of meat. And then we often increase the fat count by using oils in the cooking process. Each tablespoon of oil delivers about 130 calories and about 14 grams of fat. So if you remove a tablespoon of oil from a recipe, you reduce the calorie and fat count. You can do even more by replacing oils high in saturated fat with olive or canola oil, which are sources of monounsaturated fats—"good" fats.

Fat shows up in a lot of places, not just in oils, but also cheese, eggs, and various milk products. On top of that, many meats, especially the red ones, contain an extra glob or two (or ten) of fat. It can be a bit of a minefield. You should take care to keep the percent of calories obtained from fat under 30 percent.

I try to substitute lower-fat products whether I'm cooking at home or on the trail. In the recipes for this edition, I have replaced most oils used solely for lubrication (not for flavor) with a nonstick cooking spray like Vegalene or Pam. The skin usually is off the bird (or removed when served), and I recommend using "Select" grade beef whenever possible, and trimming any visible fat from all meats. I use 95 percent lean hamburger, and often use turkey or soy products instead of sausage, ham, and ground beef. I cook with reduced-fat cheese (made from 2 percent milk), and nonfat powdered milk. I often employ nonfat egg substitutes, too.

The result is that, if you follow my suggestions, a good portion of the recipes in this book will work well for hikers trying to keep their dietary fat counts closer to 20 percent of calories. I have marked recipes generating between 20 and 30 percent of their calories from fat with a **Ʊ**; a **ƱƱ** means that the recipe generates less than 20 percent of its calories from fat per serving.

Power Buying

Since you'll be feeding yourself—the single most important guest at your outdoor table—don't cut corners on the
quality of the food you purchase.

Fresh is always best, but there are times to use tinned or
retort (vacuum-sealed in foil pouches) packaged meats,
dried fruits and vegetables, or other prepared foods to
facilitate your efforts. Just remember that whatever packaging you carry in, you also have to carry out. That means
cans, wrappers, foils, and the like. Avoid recipes that
demand out-of-season vegetables or other exotic items.

As for meats, you might make friends with a good
butcher. They tend to carry slightly better, though more
expensive, cuts of meat, and you're better assured that the
meat is fresh, not previously frozen.

In the past few years, chicken and tuna packed in vacuum-sealed softpacks have become available. The 3.5- or
7-ounce packages offer an excellent and convenient alternative for backpackers. They don't require refrigeration
and provide portion control as well.

Vegetables and fruits should always be ripe but firm.
Even in the best of conditions, you'll be stressing them to
the limit before they are consumed. An extra day in a pack,
even tucked close by a frozen chuck of beef, can mean the
difference between green beans almondine and squirrel
food.

You'll see in the recipe chapters that I've made every
effort to eliminate partial vegetables in this edition. Thus,
"½ medium onion" has become "1 small onion." I estimate
the size of the vegetables as follows: a "small" vegetable
will fit in the palm of an adult hand, a "medium" vegetable is the size of an average adult fist, and anything
bigger is "large." As for root veggies like carrots, use
your judgment.

Powdered milk is an acceptable substitute for fresh
when mixed in a ratio of 1 part powder to 3 parts water.
Generally, though, I mix an entire packet of powder

(designed to make 1 quart of milk) with 1 to 2 cups of water, depending on how thick I want the end result. It works fine in the recipes, and leftovers taste great in coffee. Unless you are depending on the milk fat for use in a sauce (evaporated milk may then be the only solution), powdered milk cooks well.

Cheese, however, is the greatest invention to make sure you get enough milk protein and fat. When on the trail, I can't get enough cheese. It keeps well and doesn't take up much space. But, as noted above, I now use cheese made with 2 percent milk whenever possible.

The "when" in shopping is just as important as the "what." Meats should be bought at least two days in advance to allow for freezing (see next section). Fruits and veggies can wait until the day before or, even better, the morning you leave. Most food stores restock throughout the day but tend to get their shipments early. The first fruits and vegetables on display in the morning most likely will be fresher than the ones that are restocked later in the day.

GETTING THE SHOW READY FOR THE ROAD

Creativity plays a big role when you're packing in a confined space. Repackaging, with a concentration on maintaining freshness and avoiding food poisoning, is a priority.

I use a Tupperware bread carrier as my primary food locker. It's big enough to hold 12,000 or so calories in the form of meat, eggs, veggies, drinks, sugars, and . . . well, enough food for three days for my small army of cells. This box (see photo) has a nice airtight top that seals in the food and seals out some of the nastiness that courses through a pack in a given day. It won't keep your food germ free—you have to do that—but it should keep the bugs and other critters out of it long enough for you to make a stew. There are also "bear-proof" canisters available that will do the same job.

The box won't maintain temperature, but I've found a way to keep meats (beef, poultry, pork) for 24 to 36 hours. First I plan my menus and determine what cuts of meat I'll need and in what weights. I then wrap each piece in heavy-duty, freezer-thickness aluminum foil and park the package in the deep freeze for two days. Then, about 10 minutes before I toss the pack into the trunk of my car, I pull the meat out of the freezer and wrap it in another layer of foil—loosely this time to leave some air space. Then into the box it goes. There it will stay and keep, thawing as I go down the trail. It also helps keep other items in the box cool. If you want to eliminate that concern altogether, go with canned or softpack meats.

Packaging Ideas

If you look for them, you'll find an incredible number of condiments packed in single-serving packets. Items such as soy sauce, ketchup, mustard, honey, and mayonnaise are packed so that they require no refrigeration and little

The Tupperware breadbox, a backpack pantry.

space. Find these condiments (even if you have to use left-overs from your local fast-food emporium) and pack them away.

Other items demand more creative solutions. Oils can be remeasured into vials, squeeze bottles, or even baby bottles. Flour, baking powder, pancake mix, and other dry ingredients can be measured into plastic bags and sealed. Remember to label them!

Vegetables often come in their own wrappers. So do some fruits. That's what makes fresh food so easy to handle.

Eggs require some cushioning to absorb shock, but the bigger problem is to avoid crushing them if your load shifts. When I take eggs, I put them in either a small, sealed food storage container or a special egg carrier.

Rice and pasta can be cooked at home and packaged in a plastic bag. A light touch of oil mixed into the pasta or rice immediately after taking it off the stove will keep it from turning into a clump.

Again, most of this comes under the heading of common sense.

THE ONE-PAN MENU

Usually I'm on the trail for four meals, sometimes five. The four standard repasts are Saturday breakfast, lunch, and dinner, and Sunday breakfast. Sometimes I consider a late snack or dinner on Friday night.

I'm pretty generous with myself when planning my food. I tend to overplan, ending up with a fuller belly than I might normally want. Then again, you never know when you might get stuck by weather in a high ridge shelter for an extra day. The additional food will be welcome.

Before we move on to a sample menu, I'd like to offer a lunch suggestion. For a lot of trekkers, lunch is a brief break, just long enough to let muscles relax, feet cool, and to read maps. That might not leave enough time to cook a meal and clean up afterward. Here's a solution that tastes great and provides ample high-quality calories to keep you going until dinner. I picked up this updated version of historic voyageur fare as an adult leader on Boy Scout Canoeing High Adventures in Minnesota and Ontario, and it keeps a group of teenage boys going. It is frequently lunch for five of the nine days we are out in the Boundary Waters. (My thanks to those fine folks who introduced me to this recipe and made our trip, and hundreds of others every year, enjoyable and memorable.)

Prepare this at home. Cut and wrap as many pieces as you want to carry.

HUDSON BAY BREAD

¾ cup (1½ sticks) butter or margarine
1 cup sugar
3 tablespoons Karo syrup
3 tablespoons honey
½ teaspoon maple flavoring
⅓ cup ground nuts (any combination)
4 cups uncooked old-fashioned oatmeal

Cream together the first five ingredients. Combine the nuts and oatmeal and then mix with the creamed mixture. Spread in a preheated and greased 9-by-9-by-2-inch baking pan. (Press mixture down to a thickness of about 1½ inches.) Bake at 325°F for 25 minutes (check at about 20 minutes to prevent burning). When bread is done, remove from oven and immediately press down firmly with spatula. Cut into serving sizes (approximately 4-inch squares) while still warm. Makes 4 servings.

Serve this topped with peanut butter and jelly. You'll have a cold lunch that tastes great and is very filling. One slice should do it. You can substitute Hudson Bay Bread for any lunch you want.

Tip: For a double batch, use a 10-by-13-inch pan.

Sample Weekend Menu

Here's a sample of a typical weekend trip menu (and a shopping list—see next page) that includes a cooked lunch and uses a frying pan (see the appendix for weekend menus using a pot and an oven).

Saturday Breakfast
coffee
sliced oranges
Vegetable Eggs (see page 42)

Saturday Lunch
juice mix
Parmy Shrooms 'n' Noodles (see page 66)
pear, apple, or melon slices

Saturday Dinner
sliced tomato
Hair-Raisin Curry Beef or Chicken Scallopine (see pages 76 and 52)
rice
Coconuts to You Fruit Cup (see page 81)

Sunday Breakfast
coffee
juice mix
ham slice
Apple Pancakes or Huevos and Tacos (see pages 47 and 44)

Repackage the meat, cheeses, milk, and flour. Precook the noodles and spaghetti and repackage. You can also take along various snacks and hot drinks (coffee, hot chocolate, V-8 Juice). The key is to get plenty of calories to keep up your energy, which, incidentally, preserves your body core temperature so you don't get chilled as easily.

CLEANUP

One of the big chores after any meal is washing the dishes and putting away the food. Roll up your sleeves. It's time to pay for your dinner.

SHOPPING LIST

Provisions (staples)
coffee
juice mix
milk (powdered)
hot chocolate mix
wine
flour
nonstick cooking
    spray
salt
pepper (black and
    white)
sugar (white,
    brown, sugar
    subst.)

Carbs
rice (small pkg.)
potatoes (2 med.)
tortillas (4)
breadcrumbs
    (small pkg.)
noodles (1½ cups)
spaghetti or other
    pasta (2 cups)
Bisquick (¾ cup)

Proteins
eggs (11)
ham (½ cup diced,
    1 slice)
sirloin (¾ lb.)
chicken breasts (2)
cheese (¼ lb.
    Muenster, ⅓ cup
    diced other, ¼
    cup grated Par-
    mesan)

Vegetables/Fruits
oranges
pears
black olives
    (2 tbsp.)
apples
bananas
melon
raisins (½ cup)
tomatoes
green peppers (2)
onions (3)
mushrooms (9)
avocado (1)
garlic (1 clove)

Fats/Oils
peanuts (⅓ cup
    unsalted)
peanut oil (1 tbsp.)
olive oil (3 tbsp.)
butter or marga-
    rine (2 tbsp.)
shortening
    (1 tbsp.)

Sweeteners/Spices
coconut (¼ cup)
maple syrup
    (½ cup)
chicken and beef
    bouillon cubes
    (1 ea.)
Tabasco sauce
    (dash)
curry powder
    (½ tbsp.)
cinnamon (½ tsp.)
nutmeg (½ tsp.)

There should be a small vial of chlorine bleach in the
kitchen kit along with some dish soap (a biodegradable
brand if possible). Here's where you put it to work.

First, scrape your cooking vessel clean of all food debris.
(You might have done that already when you were dig-

ging for seconds or thirds.) But don't toss it, eat it! On the trail there's no garbage unless it's inedible, such as a banana peel. All of it is needed calories (read: fuel). Besides, dumping it in the woods attracts four-legged guests. Carry spoiled food out with you.

Now boil some water (carried from home or gathered and filtered/purified); remember, boiling and bleach may not affect *Giardia*, so use a filter (see pages 11–12 for more on filters) in your coffeepot. Pour some hot water into your cook pot. Add a few drops of dish soap and a little cold water. Scrub your cooking utensils first. Then the pot. Pour the soapy water out in the woods, at least 100 feet from any stream or pond.

Using the rest of your hot water, rinse your pot and utensils clean of any remaining soapy residue. You might want to grip the pan with your hot-pot tongs or gripper handle to keep from burning your hand. Dump the water in the woods as before.

Now add fresh cold water to the pot, making sure your utensils are inside. Add a few drops of bleach to kill any germs. Swish the water over all parts of the pot and utensils. Dump it as before. Air dry all. Pack away when finished.

A Clean Site Is a Happy Site

The view of your site should be just as pleasant as the view you have when you look away from your camp. After dinner take a few moments to pick up your gear, putting what you don't need for the night back in your pack. The last thing you want to leave unpacked is food. Especially in your tent!

Almost any place worth camping in comes equipped with a full complement of night-foraging critters. Most are small, like chipmunks, but they are still worthy of the nickname "minibears." They can rip a pretty big hole in a pack. Some, however, are the size of a small car, and are capable of sniffing out tasty morsels even if they are in a

tent next to a smelly human. If you don't want a bear
trashing your tent or your gear, get your food up and out
of the way.

This is where rigging a bear bag comes in handy. With
50 feet of line, you can keep your food box in one piece for
breakfast.

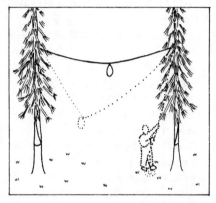

*Line is placed over branches before attach-
ing food bag.*

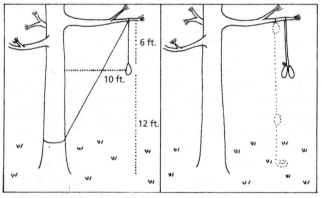

*Food bag may be hung from   Counterbalance system; retrieve
long, strong branch.   using a stick.*

The bear bag.

Locate two trees about 20 to 25 feet apart. Throw one end of the line over a branch about 12 to 14 feet off the ground on one tree (tying a rock to the end if necessary). Secure to the tree with a couple of half hitches or a clove hitch (any good locking knot will do). At the other tree, throw the other end of the line over a branch about the same height off the ground, allowing the line between the trees to sag to the ground for the moment. Tie the food bag to the line midway between the trees, then take up on the second end to remove the sag from the line and hoist the food bag as high as possible off the ground. Tie off the end.

That's the simplest method to describe, but there are any number of variations. If you really want to be fancy, use two lines and a pulley. Remember to put everything aromatic in the bear bag, including food, toothpaste, suntan lotion, and tobacco.

A quick comment. Some outdoors cookbook authors suggest chilling food in streams overnight. It's a neat idea, if there isn't any wildlife around. But my oddsmaker says the chances are pretty good that a varmint will eat your pudding well before you do.

THE FRYING PAN

So far, we've talked about the various pots, pans, kettles, ovens, and other paraphernalia you can lug along to make sure you're well fed on the trail. In this chapter, we'll get down to the brass tacks of eating.

As mentioned earlier, for those seeking lower-fat alternatives, recipes with between 20 and 30 percent of their calories generated from fat (per serving) are marked with a ◐; those with fewer than 20 percent fat calories are marked with a ◐◐.

BREAKFAST

Most of us fondly remember the smell of thick-cut bacon sizzling in a pan and the aroma of fresh-brewed coffee. Breakfast is the most important meal on the trail, as far as I'm concerned. It's what gives you the old get-up-and-go. So eat hearty and walk on!

Eggs

Scrambled eggs are probably the most basic form of trail eggs going. It means never having to say you're sorry for broken yolks. You can spruce up scrambled eggs in any number of ways, with additions of meat, cheese, and/or spices. Here's how I make mine.

And, if you want to put a big dent in the fat count (and calories, too) of any of the following dishes that call for beaten eggs, replace the hard-shell variety with a nonfat egg product like Egg Beaters. You can freeze Egg Beaters.

The carton will thaw as you hike, ready for that special Sunday breakfast or whatever. They're pasteurized so you can be secure about bacteria. Two ounces of Egg Beaters equal 1 egg, so 1 cup will replace 4 eggs.

Note: All recipes make two servings unless otherwise indicated.

SPRUCED-UP SCRAMBLED EGGS

4 to 5 large eggs
¼ cup milk (fresh, or from powdered)
salt and pepper to taste
nonstick cooking spray
extras (see following list)

Beat eggs, milk, salt, and pepper in a bowl. Spray frying pan and heat over medium heat. Pour eggs into pan and let cook undisturbed for about 30 seconds. Add desired extra ingredients and mix in with spatula. Cook for 2 minutes, scraping bottom of pan as you continue to turn the eggs until dry (or as done as you like). Eat with a hard roll, fruit, and beverage.

EXTRAS

Meat	Cheese	Spices
diced ham or steak	diced block cheese	Tabasco sauce
sliced hot dog, bologna, or salami	cubed cream cheese	oregano
chicken chunks		basil

If you're an egg fanatic, there are ways to make the dependable, edible egg more exciting. Try adding dried mushrooms, parsley, onions, or green peppers. Or put crunch into your meal with walnuts, cashews, or peanuts. And if you're really adventurous, add dried fruits, such as apricots, along with nuts.

Sometimes you have to make an even bigger meal out of breakfast. Spicing things up while getting something a bit more substantial into your stomach can make a dark and damp morning bright indeed.

VEGETABLE EGGS

 nonstick cooking spray
 2 medium potatoes, peeled and chopped (¾ cup or so)
 ½ cup green pepper, chopped
 1 small onion, chopped
 salt and pepper to taste
 4 eggs
 ⅓ cup diced cheese (use reduced fat if you want; optional)
 2 tablespoons breadcrumbs (optional)

Spray frying pan and heat over medium heat. Sauté vegetables until browned but not crisp. Add salt and pepper to taste. Break eggs over vegetable mixture and cover pan. Lower heat and cook until eggs are to your liking. Sprinkle with cheese and breadcrumbs, if desired.

And if you want to be a bit more ethnic with your eggs, consider these three egg dishes. You'll think you're walking around the Mediterranean when you taste them.

EGGS À LA HAIFA

 ¼ pound kosher salami, sliced
 1 teaspoon olive oil
 5 eggs
 salt and pepper to taste
 1 teaspoon peanut oil

Notch edges of salami slices so they won't curl while cooking. Preheat frying pan, add olive oil, and cook salami slowly. Turn once so that each side is crispy. Remove from heat and drain oil. In small bowl, beat eggs and season as desired with salt and pepper. Add peanut oil to pan and heat. Return salami slices to pan and add eggs. Fry slowly, as for an omelet, until bottom is golden brown and top is firm. Slide out of pan onto plate and flip back into pan to brown top. Watch carefully to avoid burning.

FLOR-EGG-ENZO

2 teaspoons olive oil
1 medium onion, diced
pinch of salt
¼ teaspoon pepper
1 large tomato, chopped
½ cup dried peas, rehydrated
¼ cup water
4 eggs
3 tablespoons grated Parmesan cheese
chunks of French or Italian bread (optional)

Preheat frying pan and add oil. Sauté onion until tender. Lower heat and add salt (if desired), pepper, and tomato. Simmer for about 10 minutes. Add peas and water and simmer another 10 minutes. Carefully break eggs into mixture in pan as you would for poached eggs. Continue cooking over low heat for another 15 minutes without stirring. Sprinkle with Parmesan. If desired, gently add the chunks of bread to mixture about 10 minutes before serving to soak up a bit of sauce and thicken things.

HUEVOS AND TACOS

  4 flour tortillas
  4 eggs
  4 ounces Muenster cheese (use reduced fat if you want),
      diced or grated
  dash of Tabasco sauce
  nonstick cooking spray
  1 avocado, diced
  2 tablespoons black olives, diced
  salsa (optional)

Warm tortillas in dry frying pan; set aside in covered dish to keep warm. In a bowl, scramble eggs and mix in cheese and hot sauce. Spray pan and add scrambled egg and cheese mixture. When done, remove from heat and stir in avocado and olives. Spoon onto warm tortillas, roll, and top with salsa (if desired).

I guess you could say that omelets are scrambled eggs that have a sense of togetherness. You can customize your omelets any way you wish, but if you don't cook them right from the start, you might as well make scrambled eggs.

OMELET À LA TERRY RODRIGUEZ

  1 teaspoon each olive oil, vegetable oil
  1 small potato, sliced (leave peel on)
  1 small onion, chopped
  2 or 3 eggs
  small handful pimento-stuffed olives, sliced
  pepper to taste

Heat frying pan over medium heat. Heat oils in pan and cook potatoes and onion until tender. Remove veggies from pan with slotted spoon. Beat eggs and olives together with pepper. Pour in pan and cook over low heat until partially cooked. Slide spatula around the edges periodically to loosen from pan. Add onion and potato and fold omelet. Cook until firm. Serves 1.

DON'S BASIC OMELET

    2 or 3 large eggs
    1 tablespoon water
    nonstick cooking spray

Gently beat eggs to break yolks, but don't blend completely. Add water and beat until froth begins to build. Spray pan and heat over medium heat. Pour eggs into pan slowly, allowing them to spread evenly across bottom of pan. Rotate pan gently to build a lip around edge. Cook slowly until top is firm and bottom is lightly browned. Add desired extras (diced or shredded meat, cheese, veggies, or whatever) to half of omelet. Loosen omelet from pan by gently sliding spatula underneath. Slowly slide omelet half out of pan onto plate, then flip remaining half over to close omelet. The heat of the eggs will melt the cheese and heat veggies and meat. Serves 1.

You can, of course, cook your eggs in a variety of ways, from frying to poaching. (If you can't figure out fried eggs by now, well . . .)

Did you know you can poach eggs in a frying pan? Serve them on toast over a slice of ham and cheese, if you like.

POACHED EGGS

    1½ cups water
    2 teaspoons vinegar (cider, wine, or white)
    4 eggs

Boil water in frying pan. Add vinegar and gently break eggs into lightly rolling water. (Depending on pan size, you may not be able to cook all 4 eggs at once.) As eggs solidify, roll them with a serving spoon to keep tendrils from spreading. When cooked to taste (I like about 4 to 5 minutes), remove from pan with slotted spoon.

Then again, eggs of another sort can include the easiest way I know to combine scrambled eggs and maple syrup.

FRENCH TOAST

  4 eggs
  4 to 6 slices bread, slightly stale
  nonstick cooking spray
  maple syrup, jelly, or powdered sugar (optional)

  Preheat frying pan over medium heat. In a bowl, beat eggs. Dip bread slices (you can make them stale by just leaving them out in the air for about a half hour) and soak in egg mixture until thoroughly moist. Spray pan and cook one or two slices (depending on pan size) at a time. Brown well and cook thoroughly before flipping. Remove to plate and serve with favorite topping.
  French toast works best with slightly thicker bread slices—some call it "Texas Toast" thickness.

Cakes: Griddle, Pan, and Otherwise

Sometimes eggs just aren't what you want. You want an old-fashioned trail breakfast that'll stick to your ribs all day long. Pioneers called them johnnycakes. Whatever you name them, they're fun to cook and sooo good to eat.

PANCAKES IN A SACK

  1½ cups all-purpose flour
  2 teaspoons white or yellow cornmeal
  2 teaspoons brown sugar
  ¾ teaspoon salt
  1½ teaspoons baking soda
  2 teaspoons baking powder
  2 eggs
  2 cups milk
  nonstick cooking spray

Mix the dry ingredients at home and place in a bag. At your campsite, mix all ingredients together in bowl using a whisk until blended but still lumpy. Preheat and then spray frying pan. Spoon batter into pan, enough for 2 or maybe 3 pancakes. Fry until golden brown; flip and cook other side. Serve with maple syrup and bacon or sausage.

You can also take the basic pancake recipe and add blueberries, bananas, or other fruit. And then there are some really ambitious ways to present the basic pancake.

APPLE PANCAKES

  2 to 3 apples, cored, peeled, and chopped
  ½ cup maple syrup
  2 tablespoons vegetable oil
  2 cups milk (fresh, or from powdered)
  2 eggs
  1 tablespoon liquefied Crisco shortening
  ¾ cup Bisquick
  ½ teaspoon cinnamon
  ½ teaspoon nutmeg

Combine apples, maple syrup, and oil in hot frying pan over medium heat and cook until tender. Mix milk, eggs, Crisco, Bisquick, cinnamon, and nutmeg to make batter. Remove apples from frying pan (reserve liquid) and add fruit to batter. Spoon batter into hot frying pan—you will have one large pancake. Cover pan and reduce heat. When dry bubbles appear, turn once, cover, and cook until golden brown. Serve with reserved liquid from apples. Serves 3 or 4, depending on appetite.

LUNCH AND DINNER

You can load up on food whenever you like in whatever level of complication you wish. We'll just divide things up by protein source starting with fowl things.

Poultry

You can substitute any type of bird in recipes calling for chicken as far as I'm concerned—duck, pheasant, game hen, or turkey. Some have a stronger flavor than others, so consider that before substitutions are made. Also, to keep fat under control, use skinless white meat whenever possible.

There are actually a couple of ways you can go in terms of chicken. I suggest you buy your chicken fresh. Since most stores don't package poultry in convenient single-serving sizes, you will have to repackage before your trip. The problem is that much of the chicken you find on the meat counter has been frozen at least once (if it is not frozen when you buy it). To thaw, repackage, and refreeze is a real no-no, because the moment meat is thawed, germs start to grow, and they continue to grow until the meat is refrozen completely. While the chicken is thawing in your pack, the germs can flourish again. Your meal could be spoiled before you get the chance to cook it, and your stomach could be, too, if you cook and eat spoiled meat.

If you don't want to worry about repackaging, freezing, and thawing, there is another solution. Tyson and Valley Fresh have introduced 7-ounce soft packages of precooked and diced chicken breasts that require no chilling and no cooking. Other producers will probably follow suit. These softpacks will yield two 3½-ounce servings (a bit small, but adequate). The recipes here (even those specifying "whole" chicken) will turn out fine using either source. Simply substitute the contents of one softpack for two chicken breasts. Canned chicken is another possibility, but be aware it tends to have a higher sodium count than fresh chicken, which may impact some dietary restrictions, so it's worth checking the label.

Given good-quality meat, poultry can make for some very interesting and satisfying trail meals.

Note: Technically, a whole chicken breast really offers two servings. A whole breast looks something like a valentine heart. A single serving should be slightly smaller than your hand (or half a "heart"), weighing (boneless and skinless) about 4 to 6 ounces. Thus, when I specify "two chicken breasts," I am calling for two single-serving-size pieces.

WALNUT CHICKEN

2 tablespoons vegetable oil
1 cup walnuts
1 tablespoon cornstarch
2 tablespoons cold water
2 tablespoons soy sauce
2 boneless, skinless chicken breasts
1 chicken bouillon cube
¾ cup boiling water
1 cup precooked rice

Heat oil in frying pan over high heat. Fry walnuts lightly (do not brown); remove from pan and set aside. Remove pan from heat and reserve oil. Mix cornstarch, cold water, and soy sauce with oil and pour into cool pan. Heat mixture, add chicken, and brown on both sides. Dissolve bouillon cube in boiling water and add to pan. Stir in walnuts. Continue stirring until chicken is cooked and sauce is thick. Serve over precooked rice. You could add slices of green pepper after browning chicken, if you like.

If you want an Asian flavor (you can even use a wok), there are a lot of different chicken dishes that will spice up your dinner.

ʊʊ **PODS 'N' BIRDS**

  2 boneless chicken breasts (or softpack), cut in 1-inch
      pieces
  ¼ cup cornstarch
  1 egg white
  2 tablespoons white wine
  2 teaspoons peanut oil
  4 mushrooms, sliced
  ½ to ¾ cup fresh snow peas (a good handful)
  ¼ teaspoon salt (optional)
  ¼ teaspoon ginger
  ¼ cup nuts (any kind)
  ¼ cup watercress (optional)
  1 cup precooked rice

Dredge chicken in cornstarch. Combine egg white and wine. Beat well and set aside. Heat 1 teaspoon oil in frying pan until it smokes. Sauté mushrooms, snow peas, ginger, and salt (if desired) for 2 minutes. Remove from pan with slotted spoon. Add remaining oil to pan. Add chicken to egg-white mixture in bowl. Add to pan and sauté for about 2 minutes. Add nuts and any additional vegetables you like, such as watercress, and cook about 3 to 4 minutes more. Serve with rice.

ʊʊ **DELHI CHICKEN WITH RICE**

  1 tablespoon canola oil
  1 medium onion, chopped
  2 boneless chicken breasts, cut in 1-inch cubes
  1 tablespoon flour
  ¼ teaspoon ginger
  1 to 2 tablespoons curry powder (or to taste)
  2 tablespoons honey

2 tablespoons soy sauce
2 chicken bouillon cubes
2 cups water
¾ cup uncooked white rice
1 or 2 carrots, sliced

Heat oil in pan. Add onion and sauté until brown. Add chicken and brown. Sprinkle flour, ginger, and curry powder into pan and stir. Add honey, soy sauce, bouillon cubes, and water. Simmer for 5 minutes. Add rice and carrots. Stir and simmer uncovered for another 20 to 25 minutes.

The following is a variation on the previous recipe that presents a little different flavor.

ʊʊ BOMBAY BREAST

2 boneless chicken breasts (or softpack), cut in 1-inch cubes
¼ cup soy sauce
2 tablespoons lime juice
1 tablespoon honey
¼ teaspoon curry powder
1 small green pepper, chopped
1 small red pepper, chopped
½ cup bean sprouts
1 tablespoon peanut oil

In a bowl, mix all ingredients except oil. Marinate for 20 minutes. Heat pan over high flame until very hot (a drop of water on pan surface should "dance"). Drain marinade. Stir-fry ingredients in pan for about 5 to 10 minutes or until chicken is cooked through and veggies are tender. If you wish to use the marinade as a sauce, you *must* (for food safety) bring it to a boil in the frying pan after the meat and vegetables are removed.

ʘʘ HONEY CURRY CHICKEN

  nonstick cooking spray
  ¼ cup honey
  1 tablespoon curry powder
  2 boneless chicken breasts

  Spray pan and heat over medium flame. Rub honey and
then curry powder on chicken. Add chicken to frying pan
and brown on both sides. Reduce heat, cover, and cook
for 15 minutes or until meat is done.

  Then again, maybe your taste is more Mediterranean
than Bengali.

ʘ CHICKEN SCALLOPINE

  ¼ cup flour
  salt and pepper to taste
  1 egg
  2 boneless chicken breasts (or softpack), cut in 1-inch
      cubes
  1 to 2 tablespoons olive oil
  1 clove garlic, peeled and sliced
  1 chicken bouillon cube
  ¾ cup boiling water
  ¼ cup dry red wine (or grape juice)
  4 mushrooms, sliced
  2 cups precooked spaghetti or pasta

  Place flour, salt, and pepper in plastic bag. In a bowl,
beat the egg. Dip chicken into egg and then place in bag
with flour. Shake until well coated. Heat oil in pan and
sauté garlic until it begins to brown. Lower heat, add
chicken, and sauté slowly until brown. Add bouillon cube,
water, wine, and mushrooms. Simmer uncovered for 15
minutes. Add pasta and heat through.
  Tip: You can substitute veal cutlets for the chicken.

BASIL CHICKEN SCALLOPINE

This recipe is identical to the previous one except that you substitute sliced fresh basil leaves (6 or 7, or as many as you like) for the garlic. To slice the leaves, stack them one on top of the other, gently roll the pile into a small cylinder (like a pencil), and carefully cut across the resulting tube. Do not brown them; wilt them in the hot oil for a moment just before adding the chicken for a more delicate flavor and aroma.

ʊ **CHICKEN CATCH-A-TORY**

½ pound boneless chicken (or softpack), white or dark pieces
salt and pepper to taste
garlic powder to taste
2 tablespoons olive oil
1 medium onion, sliced
1 medium green pepper, sliced
1 6-ounce can tomato paste
1 cup water
4 to 6 mushrooms, sliced
¼ teaspoon oregano

Coat chicken with salt, pepper, and garlic powder. Heat oil in pan. Add chicken and brown. Remove chicken. Add onion and green pepper to pan and sauté until tender. Add tomato paste, water, mushrooms, oregano, and chicken. Cover and cook for 30 minutes over medium flame.

This recipe goes well with rice, rice cakes, or bread.

HONG KONG BIRD, OR CHICKEN CRUNCH

2 tablespoons peanut oil
½ pound boneless chicken (or softpack), white or dark pieces
½ cup orange juice
½ teaspoon ginger
½ cup raisins
1 6-ounce can water chestnuts, sliced
½ cup white wine
½ cup salted cashews
1 tablespoon cornstarch
2 tablespoons water

Heat oil in pan. Add chicken and brown. Reduce heat and add remaining ingredients except cashews, cornstarch, and water. Simmer for 30 minutes. Add cashews. Using whisk, mix cornstarch and water in cup and add as needed to thicken sauce.

Apples are one of the easiest fruits to pack. They come with their own packaging and are 100 percent biodegradable.

↻ HENS 'N' APPLE

2 teaspoons vegetable oil
1 Cornish hen, quartered
salt and pepper to taste
½ teaspoon garlic powder
1 small onion, chopped
¼ cup dry white wine
1 medium apple (McIntosh, Granny Smith, or other tart apple), chopped

Preheat pan, add oil, and brown hen. Sprinkle with salt, pepper, and garlic powder, then add onion. Add wine and cover. Simmer for 10 minutes. Stir in apple and cover again. Cook another 10 minutes or until apples are quite soft. You can add a few small white potatoes with the wine for added carbohydrates.

Here's an old favorite.

CHICKEN À LA KING

1/3 cup water
2 boneless chicken breasts (or softpack), diced
2 tablespoons butter
1 small green pepper, chopped
3 mushrooms, sliced
2 tablespoons flour
1 cup milk
1/4 teaspoon salt (optional)
pepper to taste
1 egg yolk, slightly beaten

In preheated pan, heat water to rolling boil. Place chicken in water to poach. Stir meat constantly to avoid sticking. When tender (no more than 4 or 5 minutes), remove chicken and dispose of water. Return pan to flame and melt butter. Sauté green pepper and mushrooms. Sprinkle veggies with flour and stir. Add milk and seasonings. Cook until thick, stirring constantly. Add chicken and egg yolk. Cook another 10 minutes over medium heat, stirring to keep from scorching. Serve over bread, biscuits, or other grain.

TRIPLE C (CHICKEN, CARROTS, AND CORN)

2 tablespoons olive oil
3 cloves garlic, crushed
2 boneless, skinless chicken breasts
1 cup chicken broth (or 1 low-sodium bouillon cube dissolved in 1 cup water)
¼ teaspoon dried basil
2 medium carrots, sliced (or equivalent freeze-dried and rehydrated)
¾ cup rehydrated freeze-dried corn
2 tablespoons butter or margarine
2 tablespoons flour
½ cup water

Warm pan over medium flame. Add oil and garlic, cooking about 1 minute. Add chicken and brown 5 minutes per side. Add chicken broth and sprinkle basil over chicken. Poach for about 10 minutes, turning once. Add carrots and corn. (If the corn has not been rehydrated, add enough water to prevent corn from absorbing all the broth.) Simmer until tender, adding water (or broth) as needed. Be careful, though, not to create a chicken stew. Using slotted spoon, remove chicken and veggies to cook kit plate. Increase heat to bring remaining broth mixture to boil. Melt butter in the simmering broth. Mix flour and water in cup and gradually add to pan to thicken the broth, stirring quickly to avoid lumps. Serve sauce over plated chicken and vegetables.

BASIL WRATHBONED CHICKEN

¼ cup flour
salt and pepper
2 boneless chicken breasts
¼ cup olive oil
1 tablespoon green onion, chopped
½ cup green beans (fresh or reconstituted freeze-dried), sliced

1 chicken bouillon cube
½ cup water
1 large tomato, chopped
½ teaspoon basil
1 tablespoon vegetable oil
1 cup precooked pasta
grated Parmesan cheese (optional)

Combine flour, salt, and pepper in bowl. Dredge chicken in flour mixture. Preheat pan and add half the olive oil. Add chicken and cook until tender. Discard oil. Add remaining olive oil to pan. Sauté green onion and beans for 1 to 2 minutes. Add bouillon cube, water, tomato, and basil. Simmer uncovered for 5 minutes. Remove from pan. Add vegetable oil and precooked pasta to pan to reheat it. Serve chicken over pasta and sprinkle with Parmesan.

How many peanut butter sandwiches have you faced? And how many times have you stared at that jar and wondered if there was something else you could do with it? Here's one for you. It can be served with quinoa or another grain.

STICKY CHICKEN

2 boneless chicken breasts (or softpack), cut in 1-inch cubes
¼ cup peanut butter
1 tablespoon honey
2 tablespoons soy sauce
⅛ teaspoon garlic powder
1 tablespoon lemon juice
¼ teaspoon cayenne pepper
2 small onions, chopped
1 cup water
1 tablespoon ketchup
salt and pepper to taste

Combine all ingredients in pan and cook over medium flame until chicken is done.

You'll notice that I tend to specify boneless chicken. It really doesn't make any difference, but this way you don't have to carry out the chicken bones when you're done eating. Those small bones and splinters can tear the living daylights out of some poor scavenger's gullet if you dump them in the woods.

Once in a while, I'll pack some butter instead of oils. Sometimes you need its milk-fat content for specific sauces (like the following one), although you need to be aware of the health risks of a high-fat diet. A little is all right, a lot is not.

SAUCY CHICKEN

White Sauce
2 tablespoons butter
2 tablespoons flour
1 cup milk (fresh, or from powdered)

In pan, melt butter over low heat. Blend in flour and gradually add milk and cook, stirring constantly, for 5 minutes until sauce is smooth. Set aside in cup, clean pan, and continue with the following.

2 boneless chicken breasts
1 teaspoon salt
¼ teaspoon white pepper
¼ cup (½ stick) butter
½ cup dry white wine
¾ cup white sauce
1 medium green pepper, cut in strips

Rub chicken with salt and pepper. In preheated pan over medium flame, melt half the butter and lightly brown chicken. Add wine and white sauce. Cook 20 minutes. Add remaining butter and green pepper. Cook until hot, but do not burn sauce. Serve with precooked rice or noodles if you like.

But just maybe your taste is for something a little redder.

ʊ CHICKEN PAPRI-CRASH

½ pound boneless chicken (or softpack), white or dark
   pieces
salt and pepper to taste
garlic powder to taste
2 teaspoons peanut oil
1 medium onion, thinly sliced
1 medium green pepper, cut in strips
1 medium tomato, chopped
2 chicken bouillon cubes
1 cup water
1 tablespoon paprika (Hungarian is best)
½ cup uncooked Minute Rice

Rub chicken with salt, pepper, and garlic powder. Preheat pan and add oil and chicken. Brown chicken on both sides. Add onion and green pepper and cook for 2 to 3 minutes. Add tomato, bouillon cubes, and water. Bring to boil. Add paprika and stir. Cover and cook for 10 minutes over medium heat. Five minutes before serving, add Minute Rice to simmering sauce. Cook for 1 minute and let stand 4 minutes, covered (make sure all rice is soaking in sauce, or you'll find some unexpected crunch).

There are probably a thousand ways to clog your arteries with fried chicken. Let's do it simply and then have some fun. Just be careful not to try the next few recipes in the rain. Water in hot oil spatters furiously and can easily burn you. For that matter, be careful with hot oil even when it's not raining. Hot oil can cause some of the nastiest burns an outdoorsperson will ever face.

SQUARE-ONE FRIED CHICKEN

   1 egg
   ½ cup milk
   salt and pepper to taste
   ½ cup flour
   ½ pound chicken (white or dark pieces)
   4 to 5 tablespoons vegetable oil

Beat together egg, milk, salt, and pepper. Roll chicken pieces in flour, then in egg mixture, then in flour again. Preheat pan and heat oil until it bubbles. Be very careful! Brown chicken on all sides. Cover and cook over low flame for 20 minutes or until chicken is cooked through. Remove chicken to plate and blot with paper towel to absorb excess oil.

CHICKEN GONE CRACKERS

Same as the previous recipe but substitute ¼ cup crushed saltine crackers and ¼ cup white cornmeal for the flour. Add about ¼ teaspoon of garlic powder to egg mixture. Cook as above.

LUIGI'S FRIED CHICKEN

This time you keep the flour, but add ¼ teaspoon garlic powder to the egg mixture and ½ teaspoon oregano to the flour. Also, you cook in olive oil. You can add some basil to the flour, as well.

BATTER-UP FRIED CHICKEN

Combine egg mixture and flour together to make a batter. Add flour as needed to thicken so you get an even, deep coating on your bird. You'll also want extra oil; maybe increase it to ⅓ to ½ cup. Cook uncovered.

MR. NATURAL'S FRIED FOWL

2 eggs
½ cup milk
¼ cup flour
½ cup rolled oats, Red River cereal, or other grain
salt and pepper to taste
½ pound chicken (white or dark pieces)
½ cup peanut oil

Mix eggs, milk, flour, and grain together to form a batter. If batter seems thin, add more flour. Rub salt and pepper on chicken pieces and then dip them in the batter. Preheat pan and add oil. When oil bubbles, place chicken in pan and cook thoroughly, turning periodically until tender. Remove chicken to paper towel.

CHEESY FRIED CHICKEN

1 egg
¼ cup milk
¼ teaspoon salt (optional)
¼ teaspoon pepper
1 tablespoon grated Parmesan cheese
½ pound chicken (white or dark pieces)
½ cup flour
2 tablespoons butter or margarine
3 to 4 tablespoons olive oil
3 tablespoons lemon juice
2 teaspoons whole pine nuts
1 teaspoon fresh chopped parsley

Beat egg, milk, salt, pepper, and cheese. Dredge chicken in flour, dip it in egg mixture, and dredge it in flour again. Preheat pan and add butter and oil; heat until bubbling. Add chicken and brown on all sides. Lower heat and cook until chicken is tender (maybe 20 minutes). Remove chicken. To remaining oil in pan, add lemon juice, pine nuts, and parsley. Cook for 1 minute or until nuts are browned. Pour over chicken.

Here's a foreign food that's fun to make, fun to eat, and, I think, good for you. You can cook veggies, beef, or poultry this way. I favor a mix.

TEMPURA BATTER

1 egg
¼ teaspoon salt (optional)
¼ teaspoon sugar
½ cup cold water
⅓ cup flour

Beat eggs, salt, and sugar in bowl until frothy. Continue beating while adding cold water. Add flour and mix well, but don't overdo it. The batter holds best if you can keep it cold, say by placing it in another bowl of chilled water.

You'll need a lot of oil for tempura. Depending on the size of your frying pan, you might need as little as ½ cup peanut oil to as much as 2 cups. You need enough oil so that whatever you fry in it floats. If you carried in a wok, the same rule applies. Then heat the oil until it bubbles.

You can cook any vegetable—from potatoes to squash, from broccoli to carrots—and any meat in this batter. Just make sure that your pieces (especially for solid veggies like carrots) are not too thick to fry. I suggest:

CHICKEN TEMPURA

2 boneless chicken breasts, cut in strips
1 or 2 large carrots, peeled and thinly sliced
1 large green pepper, cut in thin strips (julienned)
1 small Vidalia (sweet) onion, sliced ⅛ inch thick
1 cup precooked rice (optional)

Dip chicken and veggies into the batter a few pieces at a time and add to hot oil. Cook until lightly browned (make sure chicken is cooked through!). Remove to a paper towel to drain. Remove crumbs from oil with slotted spoon before adding next batch. Serve alone or with rice. Soy sauce is a nice touch.

Vegetables

There are a lot of folks who like to take a day off every once in a while from eating meat. Maybe a main dish that centers around something green. It's a nice change of pace and eliminates the need (usually) for radical refrigeration. Just remember that vegetables bruise easily and, when dinged, spoil fast.

⊍⊍ EGGPLANT RAGOUT

1 small eggplant, peeled and julienned
1 medium tomato, chopped
1 small onion, chopped
1 small green pepper, chopped
1 6-ounce can tomato paste
½ cup water
salt and pepper to taste
¼ teaspoon paprika
¼ teaspoon basil
grated Parmesan cheese (optional)

Put everything in a large frying pan. Stir and simmer until veggies are soft and sauce is thick, about 30 minutes. You might also add some Parmesan cheese or seasoned breadcrumbs to thicken the base.

Many times, the veggie role in a meal in the wild is as a side dish. Remember that you can usually cook any vegetables you want in the side of your frying pan—accepting the fact that you may, from time to time, have to live with a bit of unusual sauce as a complement to your greens.

ROAD HOUSE HASH BROWNS

1 tablespoon peanut oil
1 medium onion, chopped
1 large potato, thinly sliced (leave peel on)
salt and pepper to taste
leftover bacon, salami, or other meat, diced (optional)

Heat pan over medium flame and add oil. Sauté onion in oil until tender. Add all other ingredients and continue cooking until potatoes begin to stick to pan. This goes well with red meats, but fits any meal. A real belly-warmer.

MOUNTAIN FRIES

2 large potatoes, cut in ¼-inch spears (leave peel on)
1 tablespoon Tabasco sauce
¼ cup vegetable oil
seasoned salt (optional)

Place potatoes and Tabasco sauce in plastic bag and shake to coat. Heat oil in pan. Add potatoes and cook for 3 to 5 minutes, stirring occasionally to prevent sticking. Remove with slotted spoon. Drain on cloth or paper towel. Sprinkle with seasoned salt. My kind of hot!

SPUDS 'N' PEPPERS

1 jalapeño pepper, roasted and diced (watch it, these are potent)
1 tablespoon oil
1 medium green pepper, thinly sliced
1 medium red pepper, thinly sliced
2 large potatoes, peeled and thinly sliced
salt and pepper to taste
garlic powder to taste

First, you have to roast the jalapeño pepper: Devise a type of rack in the frying pan—maybe a piece of aluminum foil—to keep the jalapeño off surface of pan. Place jalapeño on rack, cover, and roast for 5 to 10 minutes over high flame. Remove pepper from pan and, when cool, peel and dice it. Place oil in pan and heat. Add all vegetables and fry until browned and crispy. Add seasonings as desired.

Tip: To make a complete meal, push the vegetables to side of pan and cook a boneless chicken breast in the juices for about l0 minutes, flipping occasionally.

TENNESSEE STIR-FRY

1 medium onion, diced
1 medium green pepper, julienned
1 tablespoon corn oil
3 medium russet potatoes, peeled and thinly sliced
½ pound precooked turkey ham, diced
black pepper to taste

Over medium flame, heat oil and cook onion and green pepper until soft. Add potatoes and brown. Add ham and stir everything until hot. Sprinkle with pepper.

For a real scrambler, add a couple of eggs (or egg powder and water)!

PARMY SHROOMS 'N' NOODLES

1 tablespoon peanut oil
5 mushrooms, diced
1 medium onion, diced
½ cup milk
1½ cups precooked noodles
½ cup ham, diced (optional)
¼ cup grated Parmesan cheese

Heat frying pan over medium heat. Add oil and sauté vegetables until tender, but not brown. Drain oil. Add milk, noodles, ham, and cheese and toss over low heat for 1 to 2 minutes until mixture is hot.

SUNSHINE SQUASH

2 tablespoons peanut oil
1 medium onion, diced
1 large summer squash, diced
5 to 6 mushrooms, sliced or chopped
¼ to ½ teaspoon garlic powder
¼ teaspoon pepper
salt to taste

Preheat frying pan over medium flame. Add oil and sauté onion until tender. Add squash and cook uncovered to desired tenderness (I like mine "crisp-tender"). Add the mushrooms and seasonings and cook for 3 to 4 minutes more.

Blanching vegetables at home is an easy way to make sure you have cooked vegetables on the trail. Usually, blanching works best with firm green vegetables such as beans, broccoli, zucchini, and pea pods. But you can shorten your cooking time with any frying-pan vegetable by taking a few minutes at home to blanch them and then repack them in a bag. They'll still be crispy, but well on their way to being cooked "just right."

To blanch, boil about 2 cups water (salt optional) in a pot. Place the desired vegetables in water and cook for 2 minutes—no more, no less. Drain immediately. Let cool and place in plastic bag. Chill in fridge.

Here's a tasty way to use those home-blanched green beans.

MCAULIFFE'S GREEN BEANS

2 tablespoons vegetable oil
3 ounces (or more) sliced almonds
1½ cups green beans, sliced (either fresh or reconstituted freeze-dried)

Heat frying pan over low flame. Add oil and let heat. Add almonds and fry gently (be careful not to burn them). Add beans and increase heat to medium. Toss beans and almonds together for about 1 minute—long enough for veggies to heat, but not long enough for almonds to burn.

STIR-FRY VEGETABLES

    3 tablespoons peanut oil
    2 cups mixed vegetables, chopped (green beans, pea
        pods, carrots, onions, mushrooms, green or red pep-
        pers)
    2 tablespoons soy sauce
    salt and pepper to taste

Heat frying pan over high flame (drop of water on surface should "jump"). Add oil and let heat. Add vegetables
and stir-fry for about 2 to 3 minutes. Add soy sauce, salt,
and pepper. Toss and stir-fry for another minute. Serve
over precooked rice or with bread.

POTATO PANCAKES

    2 large potatoes, peeled and grated
    1 egg, beaten
    1 tablespoon flour
    ½ teaspoon baking powder
    2 tablespoons butter or margarine (or nonstick cooking
        spray)

Combine all ingredients except butter and form into flat
cakes. Over medium flame, heat butter. Cook like regular
pancakes, turning to brown both sides.

QUESTADILLAS OF MANY COLORS

2 soft flour tortillas
1 2- to 3-ounce can mild green chilis, sliced or diced
¼ cup cheddar cheese (use reduced fat if you want), grated
¼ cup jack cheese (use reduced fat if you want), grated
olive oil or nonstick cooking spray
mild salsa
sour cream

Place one tortilla on wax paper and cover with as many green chilis as you like. Sprinkle with cheeses and cover with other tortilla. Press gently. Warm pan and rub surface with oil (or use cooking spray). Place quesadilla in pan and cook until lightly browned. Flip and press with spatula. Brown and cook until cheese is melted (about 3 minutes, depending on heat). Remove, cut into wedges, and serve with salsa, sour cream, and (if desired) guacamole.

Tip: For the cheeses, try using the grated "Mexican Blend" cheese you can find at your grocery store.

Meat

Yes, you can substitute bear, venison, or buffalo for beef, if you wish. But whatever meat you use, make sure that it's high quality and well trimmed to eliminate waste (bones, gristle, and fat).

Although most of the following recipes specify particular cuts, you can usually substitute any grade. In recipes calling for hamburger or ground beef, I like to use 95 percent lean. You can use lower percentages, if you don't mind figuring out where to dump the excess grease. When all else fails, go with chopped, ground, sliced, or whole top sirloin. These cuts are lean and usually tender enough for most combinations.

Often, though, you'll start out cooking with hamburger. It's forgiving of beginners and weary hikers.

❍❍ HAMBURGER HASH

½ pound ground beef
1 medium onion, diced
1 cup rehydrated pinto beans (presoaked and packed in
    plastic bag)
¼ cup ketchup
2 tablespoons brown sugar
¾ cup water
1 beef bouillon cube
salt and pepper to taste

Brown beef and add onion. Cook until tender. Add all remaining ingredients. Stir mixture and simmer for 20 to 30 minutes or until sauce is smooth.

Tip: Start soaking your beans in the morning when you are on the trail. Put them in a 32-ounce Nalgene bottle (or other wide-mouth vessel) with twice as much water as beans.

PURPLE BURGER

½ pound ground beef
1 small onion, minced
¼ cup pickled beets, diced
½ cup cooked potato, diced
¼ teaspoon salt (optional)
⅛ teaspoon black pepper
1 tablespoon butter or margarine

In bowl, gently mix all ingredients except butter. Heat frying pan over medium flame. Melt butter in pan and spoon mixture onto hot surface. Flatten with spatula to about 1 inch. Cover and cook for 3 to 5 minutes or until browned. Flip once, cover, and finish cooking for another 5 minutes or until done. Serve with hardtack or rye bread.

Sometimes you might want to make a round meal rather than a square one in your frying pan. And what better way to celebrate nature than with meatballs accompanied by hash browns? Or stir-fried green beans? Or raw sliced zucchini?

SOUPY MEATBALLS

½ pound ground beef
¼ cup seasoned breadcrumbs
½ medium onion, grated
salt and pepper to taste
2 tablespoons corn oil
2 cups water
2 packets beef-based soup mix (single-serving size)
1 cup noodles or macaroni (precooked saves time)

Combine meat, breadcrumbs, onion, and salt and pepper. Shape into meatballs about 1 to 1½ inches in diameter. Heat frying pan and add oil. Brown meatballs (roll them around to brown). Add water, soup mix, and noodles. Simmer for 5 to 10 minutes. If desired, add veggies such as diced fresh tomatoes to bubbling mix.

SWEDISH MEATBALLS

½ pound ground sirloin
¼ teaspoon sugar
1 egg
¼ teaspoon sage
¼ teaspoon allspice
¼ teaspoon nutmeg
1 small onion, finely chopped
1 cup breadcrumbs
⅓ cup cold water
1 tablespoon vegetable oil

Mix all ingredients except oil together in bowl and knead well. Shape into 1-inch meatballs. Heat oil in frying pan and brown over medium flame. Roll meatballs around until cooked through. Cover and simmer for about 20 minutes, periodically rolling meatballs. If you like, you can add sliced potato and onion before simmering.

GYPSY MEATBALLS

Same as above, but substitute uncooked Minute Rice for breadcrumbs and substitute oregano and basil (¼ teaspoon each) for sage, allspice, and nutmeg.

Everybody's mother has a recipe for goulash. Mine made it with hamburger and elbow macaroni.

◊ MOM'S GOULASH

½ pound hamburger
salt and pepper to taste
1 large onion, diced
1 large green pepper, diced
½ teaspoon oregano
¼ teaspoon garlic powder

½ teaspoon basil
1 teaspoon sugar
1 fresh tomato, cubed (optional)
1 6-ounce can tomato paste
1 cup water
1½ cups precooked macaroni

Heat frying pan over medium flame and brown meat until crumbly. Add salt, pepper, onion, and green pepper and sauté until veggies are soft. Drain any fat. Return to heat and add remaining ingredients except macaroni; stir until tomato paste is dissolved. Simmer for 10 minutes. Add macaroni and stir until hot. Serve with grated Parmesan cheese and French bread.

SMOKE BURGERS

½ pound ground sirloin
½ small onion, minced
¼ teaspoon Liquid Smoke
ground pepper to taste
garlic powder to taste
1 tablespoon vegetable oil

Combine all ingredients except oil in bowl and knead by hand until well mixed. Heat frying pan over medium flame and add oil. Shape meat mixture into two ½-inch-thick burgers and fry in pan to desired degree of doneness. If you're a cheeseburger nut, melt a thick slice of medium to sharp cheddar over each burger. Serve on a kaiser roll with salad on the side.

Sooner or later you're going to want to get away from the ground-round side of life and step up to a different slice. That's when it gets to be fun.

◑◑ TOKYO TERIYAKI

¾ pound sirloin steak, cut in 1-inch cubes
1 small onion, chopped
¼ teaspoon ginger
3 ounces teriyaki sauce
1 cup precooked rice
pineapple chunks

Combine steak, onion, ginger, and teriyaki sauce in bowl and marinate for 10 to 15 minutes. Heat frying pan and add steak and marinade. Cook until done. Add a little water, if necessary. Push meat and onions to one side of pan. Add precooked rice and heat through. About 1 minute before serving, add pineapple chunks and heat.

What hike would be complete without at least one dose of something to warm the insides and stretch the limits of your partner's patience?

CHILI BLAST

1 pound stew beef or steak, cut in ½-inch cubes
1 small onion, chopped
1 clove garlic, minced
2 tablespoons vegetable oil
½ cup freeze-dried corn, rehydrated
1 6-ounce can tomato paste
1¼ cups water
2 chili peppers (mild or hot), seeded and chopped
¼ teaspoon salt (optional)
spices to taste (cumin, coriander, or chili powder)
one or more of following (optional): raisins, grapes,
    summer squash, zucchini, cactus ears

In frying pan, cook beef, onion, and garlic in oil until beef is browned. Add all other ingredients except optional ones. Bring to boil and reduce heat. Simmer covered for about 30 minutes. Add desired optional ingredients and simmer about 10 minutes more or until meat is tender.

As for the next recipe, let me say thanks to a friend who Thai'd one on!

◑ BANGKOK BEEF 'N' PEPPERS

¾ pound sirloin, cubed
¼ teaspoon garlic
½ teaspoon ginger
½ tablespoon sugar
1 tablespoon soy sauce
¼ teaspoon cayenne pepper
1 tablespoon vegetable oil
1 medium onion, chopped
1 medium red pepper, cut in strips
1 beef bouillon cube dissolved in ¾ cup boiling water
4 to 5 large mushrooms, sliced
1 teaspoon cornstarch
1 tablespoon water
1½ cups precooked rice

In bowl, combine beef, garlic, ginger, sugar, soy sauce, and cayenne pepper. Heat frying pan over high flame until very hot. Add oil and sauté onion and red pepper until soft. Add beef and cook until browned. Stir often. Add bouillon mixture and mushrooms and cook until sauce thickens. Mix cornstarch and water in cup with whisk and add to thicken sauce. Serve with precooked rice. I've found that some sliced fresh pineapple on the plate tastes great and helps cut the sting of this dish.

HAIR-RAISIN CURRY BEEF

½ cup boiling water
½ cup raisins
1 tablespoon olive oil
¾ pound sirloin, cut in 1-inch cubes
1 medium onion, chopped
1 medium green pepper, chopped
½ tablespoon curry powder
½ teaspoon salt (optional)
⅓ cup unsalted peanuts
1 beef bouillon cube

In a dish or small bowl, pour boiling water over raisins and set aside. In frying pan, add oil and brown meat and vegetables over medium heat. Drain oil. Add curry powder and mix well. Mix in salt (if desired) and nuts. Drain raisins (reserve juice) and add to meat mixture. To reserved raisin juice, add enough water to measure ½ cup. Add this and bouillon cube to meat mixture and simmer for 15 minutes.

The following is not a recipe for the fat-conscious. However, for a trail-end meal, there are few that can match this one for the fun of cooking and the sheer enjoyment of eating. You do have to be quick with this one. Have all your ingredients prepped before you start to cook.

STIR-FRY BEEF WITH BUTTER SAUCE

Butter Sauce
1 tablespoon peanut oil
2 ounces slivered almonds
1 green onion, chopped
¼ teaspoon curry powder
1 stick butter (margarine is OK in a pinch)
juice of 1 lemon
salt and pepper to taste

Preheat frying pan over medium flame. Add oil and brown almonds and green onion. Remove from heat and drain. Wipe pan clean. Return nuts and onion to pan and add remaining ingredients. Let butter melt, but do not brown. Stir until well mixed. Remove from pan and set aside in covered bowl.

2 tablespoons peanut oil
¾ pound beef, thinly sliced
1 small green pepper, chopped
1 small red pepper, chopped
3 large mushrooms, sliced
½ teaspoon salt (optional)
pepper to taste

Heat oil until it smokes. Add meat and quickly brown. Turn regularly to keep from sticking and burning. Add remaining ingredients and quickly stir-fry. Reduce heat and add butter sauce. Toss quickly to coat.

Tip: If you'd like a lower-fat version, replace the butter sauce with ¼ cup red wine. Or, omit the butter sauce and go for some soy sauce to make tongues really tingle. By the way, all these variations work well with rice. Remember, precook the rice at home and then pour the freshly cooked food over it to reheat. If you have ample liquid, you can use uncooked Minute Rice. Remember to add water if you need it.

☉ SOY SAUCE SIRLOIN

2 tablespoons peanut oil
½ pound sirloin, thinly sliced
5 green onions, sliced in 1-inch pieces
1 6-ounce can water chestnuts, sliced
1 medium green pepper, sliced
4 ounces dried pineapple chunks
2 tablespoons cornstarch
¼ cup water
¼ cup soy sauce

Preheat pan and add oil. Sauté beef in hot oil for about 30 seconds on each side. Add remaining ingredients except cornstarch, water, and soy sauce. Cook 4 to 5 minutes over medium flame. Meanwhile, dissolve cornstarch in water. Add cornstarch mixture and soy sauce to pan and stir until thickened.

Feel like a taste of the Old West?

BIG JOHN'S DIXIE-FRIED STEAK

2 tablespoons oil
¾ pound steak, well marbled, cut into 2 pieces
¾ cup water
¼ cup flour
salt and pepper to taste

Heat oil in pan over medium flame. Add meat and slowly fry steak. Reduce heat as needed to keep from sticking. After meat is cooked as you prefer, remove from pan. Add water and slowly stir in flour to make a gravy, carefully scraping pan to remove all meat drippings. Pour gravy over steak. Serve with a raw carrot and hard rolls, or try them with Mountain Fries (page 65).

Take a hard left turn at Vladivostok to get to the next flavor classic.

BEEF STROGANOFF

¾ pound steak (round or sirloin), cut in 1-inch cubes
3 tablespoons flour
3 tablespoons corn oil
1 medium onion, chopped
1 clove garlic, minced
¼ teaspoon pepper
¼ teaspoon paprika
5 mushrooms, sliced
⅓ cup dry red wine or sherry (or grape juice)
1 packet dry creamed vegetable soup mix, reconstituted
    with water
4 ounces cream cheese (use nonfat if you want)
precooked noodles

Place beef and flour in plastic bag and shake to coat. Heat frying pan over medium to high flame. Add oil. Sauté onion and beef in oil until beef is uniformly browned. Add remaining ingredients except soup and cream cheese. Stir and let simmer for about 5 minutes. Add soup and simmer another 10 minutes. Slice in cream cheese and stir well. Dish out steaming hot over precooked noodles.

Here's a version of goulash that's sure to raise a few tent stakes whenever it's served.

◑◑ PROTEIN-BUSTER GOULASH

nonstick cooking spray
½ pound sirloin steak, cut in ½-inch cubes
2 medium onions, chopped
2 stalks celery, sliced
2 packages dry tomato soup mix (single-serving size)
1½ cups water
1 15-ounce can red kidney beans, drained
salt, pepper, and paprika to taste
flour

Spray pan and heat over medium to high flame. Add meat and brown until done. Add onions, celery, soup mix, and water. Simmer for 30 minutes. Add beans and seasonings. Thicken sauce with flour as needed. With all the beef and beans, you won't run short on protein. Serve this with bread and you'll have a meal you can really wrap yourself around.

◑ LOTS OF Ps—PESTO PORK WITH PEPPERS AND PASTA

nonstick cooking spray
½ pound pork loin cutlets
2 teaspoons prepared pesto sauce
½ cup low-sodium chicken broth
1 large green pepper, sliced in strips
1 large red pepper, sliced in strips
1½ cups precooked pasta
salt and pepper to taste

Spray pan and heat over medium flame. Rub pork with pesto and brown until cooked through. Pour in chicken broth. Stir in vegetables and sauté until tender. Add pasta and toss until warmed through. Cook for about 1 minute. Season to taste and serve.

DESSERT

I'll be honest. The frying pan isn't the easiest thing to use if you're trying to cook dessert. That's why I have a favorite fruit cup recipe.

COCONUTS TO YOU FRUIT CUP

1 orange, cubed
1 apple or pear, cubed
1 banana, sliced (optional)
¼ cup flaked coconut
1 tablespoon sugar (optional)

Mix fruit, coconut, and sugar (if desired) and let rest in a covered dish for 30 minutes. Eat with great joy.

Many cultures feature pancakes as a favorite dessert. They're usually thin, sweet, and covered with marvelous fruit preserves or powdered sugar. Any pancake batter mix can serve the purpose, but add more water or milk than suggested because you want a thin batter to give you delicate, thin pancakes.

I'm half-Swedish, so here's a family favorite from the Old Country (see next page). If you're French, you'll know these as crepes; to me, they're plättar.

PLÄTTAR

1 egg
²/₃ cup milk
dash of salt (optional)
1 tablespoon sugar
¼ cup flour
1 tablespoon vegetable oil
nonstick food spray

Beat egg well. Add milk, salt, sugar, flour, and oil. Mix thoroughly. Spray pan and heat over medium flame. Cook pancakes on both sides. If batter is too thick, add a little more milk. These pancakes should be very thin. Serve with powdered sugar or strawberry preserves.

You can use your frying pan to cook doughnuts, but I don't recommend it for two reasons. First, you have to use a lot of oil (at least 1 cup). That's both heavy to carry and difficult to dispose of when you're done. Second, and even more important, you have to bring that oil to a very high temperature. One slip and you and your trekking companions will be dealing with a very serious burn. Be safe, be smart, and keep the deep-frying to a minimum.

THE POT

Although the recipes for the frying pan are designed for quick cooking, the ones for the pot are meant to be a bit slower to finish, allowing tougher meats to tenderize, pungent flavors to mellow, and tasty sauces to blend into a savory meal.

I've found that meals built in the pot offer a unique taste experience. Certainly, the pot has traditionally been a world of stews and soups. But with a little extra effort and creativity, you can stroll down the Appian Way or peer out onto the misty moors when you put the pot on the burner.

Note: The boiling point of water drops 9°F with every 5,000 feet in altitude; thus cooking times of boiled foods double at 5,000 feet and quadruple at 10,000 feet. Remember too that some stoves (such as alcohol) cook slower than others. Adjust accordingly.

And, as mentioned earlier, recipes with fewer than 30 percent fat calories are marked with a ☻; those with fewer than 20 percent fat calories are marked with a ☻☻.

BREAKFAST

Getting breakfast out of the pot is one quick way to hit the trail. Take a look at some of these favorites. These recipes serve two unless otherwise noted.

Cereals

Cereals and other grain dishes are an easy way to get started and give you a lot of get-up-and-go. But as with all meals, you have to build a complete and balanced supply of nutrients. Don't forget the fruit and milk.

OATMEAL EXTRAORDINAIRE

 1½ cups water
 ⅛ teaspoon salt (optional)
 ⅔ cup old-fashioned oatmeal or steel-cut oats
 ½ cup raisins
 2 tablespoons brown sugar
 ¼ cup walnuts

Over a medium flame, bring the water and salt (if desired) to a boil. Add oats, stirring slowly to prevent lumps. Cook for 5 minutes (12 to 15 minutes for steel cut) or until all water is absorbed. Add raisins and cook for another 2 to 3 minutes, stirring occasionally. When ready to eat, stir in brown sugar and walnuts.

◑◑ CINNAMON-ORANGE CREAM OF WHEAT

 2 cups water
 ⅛ teaspoon salt (optional)
 ½ cup Cream of Wheat (original, not quick)
 1 teaspoon cinnamon
 1 6-ounce can mandarin orange segments, drained

Over a medium flame, bring water and salt (if desired) to a boil. Add cereal, stirring to prevent lumps. Cook for 5 minutes, making sure not to burn the cereal. Just before you're ready to eat, add the cinnamon and oranges.

Of course, you can add just about anything you want to a cooked grain mixture. Just follow package directions and then let your imagination run wild. Some of the great taste combinations I've tried in my oatmeal are apple chunks (dried or fresh), cinnamon, and nuts; dates and brown sugar; real maple syrup (needs no more help); and applesauce and sliced strawberries. Most of these additions require no cooking. Just put them in when you're ready to eat. Some, like raisins and apples, need a few minutes in the mix to soften and warm up.

There are at least a dozen different commercial hot cereals to choose from. Look for bulk cereals at better markets that cater to quality-conscious consumers. You'll save a lot of money by eliminating the marketing and packaging. For instance, by buying in bulk, you can get steel-cut oats for around 99 cents per pound. The 10-ounce aluminum can sells for more than $4. By the way, many cold cereals, such as Grape Nuts and Shredded Wheat, can be cooked to make an early-morning tummy warmer.

Morning Beverages

I like coffee. Steaming hot, strong coffee. And I'm not a fanatic who insists that the only real trail coffee has grounds and egg shells floating in it. To get around the need to deal with a coffeepot, I use a small cook pot with a tea ball to contain the coffee grounds. Makes cleanup a whole lot easier.

DON'S TRAIL BREW

2 tablespoons fresh-ground coffee (auto-drip or finer grind)
2 cups water
1 tablespoon sugar
1 teaspoon cinnamon

Bring water to boil. Spoon coffee into tea ball and add to boiling water. Let brew for 4 to 5 minutes. Remove tea ball. Add sugar and cinnamon. Makes 2 cups. Serve with milk, cream, or whitener if you prefer. For mocha, substitute unsweetened cocoa for the cinnamon.

Eggs and Meat

About any way you can cook an egg in a frying pan, you can do in a pot—a bit differently, but cooked nonetheless. It's just more interesting when you go beyond the eggs and start adding meat, for instance. And that's where you have to change the way you think about how you cook meat.

For many people, meat isn't properly prepared until there's a charred layer to prove it passed the trial by fire. But think Asian for a moment. Meat that has been steamed, not unlike dim sum, is just as well done as if it were stuck to your frying pan two or three times. That's how I cook my morning meat.

You need only about ½ cup of boiling water and a cover for your pot to fix most cuts of meat. However, it's critical that the meat is thawed, especially if it's fresh instead of precooked or left over. Otherwise, you might end up with sausage or steak that is too rare or even dangerously undercooked.

As with all foods, make sure your meat hasn't spoiled before you cook it. You usually can't tell if meat is spoiled just by looking at it, though certainly an "off" smell should

The vegetable steamer.

tell you something's wrong. But sometimes meat can be bad and not give off any telltale aroma. When in doubt, double-wrap it, pack it out with you, and toss it when you get home. Better a meal without meat than risk food poisoning.

Another caution about steaming involves handling the utensils and steering clear of the steam. You can get an incredibly nasty burn from steam. Never place the steamer in a pot of boiling water. Always start with everything cold: The meat, the steamer, the pot, the water, and even the stove. When you remove the steamer from the pot, carefully lift the cover off away from your face. The first thing out of the pot will be live steam (that's steam under pressure—and it's a lot hotter than 212°F). Then, let everything cool off for a few moments before you move in with your hot-pot tongs to remove the steamer.

And now for the recipes.

SAUSAGE LINKS

uncooked links (regular, brown 'n' serve, or soy), thawed

Place links on steamer. Pour ½ cup water in pot. Put steamer in pot and cover. Over medium flame, bring water to boil. Time cooking from when water boils; uncooked links get 10 minutes, soy or brown 'n' serve just 5.

HAM STICKS

4 ounces cooked ham, cut into 4-inch sticks

Steam until piping hot (about 5 to 8 minutes). You can substitute Spam, but the consistency of the cooked product will be different.

SOY SAUCE STEAK SUNRISE

⅓ cup soy sauce
2 tablespoons honey
½ pound sirloin or other lean steak, thinly sliced
½ cup cold water

Mix soy sauce and honey, and marinate steak in it for 15 minutes. Discard marinade. Place meat on steamer and put in pot with water. Cover and bring water to boil. Cook meat for 3 minutes (rare) to 6 or 7 minutes (well done).

A.M. SAUSAGE BURRITO

4 flour tortillas
2 tablespoons peanut oil
1 cup water
½ pound ground sausage
4 eggs
diced green pepper and onion (optional)

Rub oil on one side of each tortilla. Roll loosely and place on steamer. Place steamer in pot, add water, and bring to boil. Heat tortillas for about 1 minute. Remove pot from heat and remove cover. After steam clears, remove tortillas and place an equal amount of sausage meat in each tortilla on nonoiled side. Fold tortillas over meat so they resemble small pillows. Place back on steamer with folded part down. Bring water level back to 1 cup and place steamer inside pot. Cover and bring to boil over medium heat. Put eggs alongside tortillas on steamer to hard-boil. Time for 15 minutes once water boils. To spice up the burrito, add some diced green pepper and onion to meat before placing in tortillas.

A great staple of any wilderness breakfast is the common chicken egg, though you can also use duck or goose eggs to fill out your morning plate.

Many of us think of eggs and frying pans as inseparable.

Unfortunately that's too often the case, especially when we forget the cooking spray. But eggs in a pot have a noble history, reaching back into the smoky past of savory stews bubbling in cast-iron cauldrons set over a few chunks of aspen or chestnut.

You can always treat your pot like a frying pan and make scrambled eggs, but be adventurous and try some of these recipes that turn the benefits of the pot to your eggs' advantage.

HARD-BOILED EGGS

3 cups water
¼ teaspoon salt
4 large eggs

Pour water in pot with salt (if desired). Bring water to a rolling boil over medium to high flame. Reduce heat so water is just barely bubbling. Add eggs. Maintain flame so that water keeps boiling very slowly. Cook eggs too fast and they'll crack and ooze. Boil for about 5 to 7 minutes. (At higher altitudes—up to about 10,000 feet—cook 10 to 12 minutes.) Remove eggs with spoon and set aside to cool (soak in bowl of cold water). Peel and eat.

Hard-boiled eggs are versatile. You can peel and eat them as is. You can slice and sprinkle them with salt and pepper, grated cheese, diced chives or onions, or pine nuts and grated Parmesan. You can also do a bit more with hard-boiled eggs while still in the pot.

EGGS À LA GOLDENROD

 4 hard-boiled eggs
 ¾ cup milk (fresh, or from powdered)
 ½ to 1 cup water
 ⅓ cup flour
 white pepper
 4 slices bread

Peel eggs and separate yolks from whites. Slice whites and set aside. Over a medium flame, heat milk in pot. Do not boil. In a bowl, add water a bit at a time to flour to make a paste. Slowly add paste to milk to make white sauce (stir as mixture thickens). Add sliced egg whites. Add white pepper to taste. Heat mixture through and spoon over bread. Mash yolks and sprinkle over top.

The most popular way to cook eggs in a pot, besides boiling them, is poaching them. Poaching eggs on the trail isn't hard, it just takes a bit of wrist action.

POACHED EGGS

 2½ cups water
 ¼ cup white vinegar
 4 large eggs

Over a medium to high flame, bring water to a boil and add vinegar. With a spoon, stir liquid to create a whirl-pool. Break eggs into whirlpool while continuing to swirl the water. This will roll the eggs and keep them from spreading out. Every 15 to 20 seconds, reverse the direction of the whirlpool by rocking the pot in the opposite direction. After about 3 minutes, remove eggs from pot. Serve over bread, rolls, or hot hash.

Poached eggs are the base for the king of all egg dishes: eggs Benedict. Simply speaking, this is poached eggs on top of sliced Canadian bacon and English muffins, covered with Hollandaise sauce. It's possible to make Hollandaise sauce in the woods, but you need a double boiler and a lot of patience. I suggest substituting a spruced-up white sauce.

WHITE SAUCE FOR POACHED EGGS

2 tablespoons flour
½ cup water
½ cup milk (fresh, or from powdered)
2 tablespoons butter or margarine
salt and pepper to taste
grated Parmesan cheese (optional)

Mix flour and water in bowl to form paste. Heat milk in pot over medium flame. Add butter, stirring frequently until melted. Add flour mixture gradually to thicken sauce. Add salt and pepper. Continue to heat until sauce is thick. Set aside and cover. Serve over poached eggs placed on slice of ham or Canadian bacon on top of sliced English muffin to make mock eggs Benedict. For some added flavor, stir in a healthy dash of grated cheese.

LUNCH AND DINNER

Turning your only pot into a vat of earthly delights is easy if you're willing to take a little time. I've always found that cooking in a pot offers a totally different experience from cooking in a frying pan. The pot is a world of spices and sauces, of subtle differences in flavor, where gentle nuances bring new blendings of taste to outdoor cuisine.

A pot-based meal should be cooked slowly. You have to accept the fact that patience is the critical factor in melding meats, vegetables, seasonings, and liquids into more than an uninspired soup or stew. You can expect to spend 30 minutes or more cooking after the preparation is done. But the wait will be worth it.

Poultry

I prefer to cook with chicken breasts, but you can use any part of the bird—legs, thighs, whatever—in these recipes. You can substitute other poultry, if you like, but use caution. Turkey dark meat (legs, thighs) has a stronger flavor than chicken and will yield a different result. I suggest you use turkey breast if you want to substitute. Duck is quite greasy, so I avoid it.

Chicken is great because it cooks quickly, it's lean (if you strip away the fat and go skinless), it's packed with nutrition, and it works with just about anything you can carry. And remember the various softpacks of precooked chicken now on the market. You can substitute a 7-ounce softpack any time the recipe calls for boneless and cubed or diced meat.

Note: As mentioned in the previous chapter, two chicken breasts really mean one whole breast (which looks something like a valentine heart) cut in half. Each piece will weigh 4 to 6 ounces.

◔ ICEBOX CHICKEN WITH STUFFING

nonstick cooking spray
1 medium onion, diced
1 small green pepper, chopped
1 small tomato, diced
1 stalk celery, chopped
½ pound boneless chicken breast (or softpack), cubed
salt and pepper to taste
1 chicken bouillon cube
½ cup water
½ cup seasoned croutons, stuffing mix, or uncooked
    Minute Rice
½ teaspoon poultry seasoning, if you use Minute Rice

Over a medium flame, heat pot. Spray pot and sauté vegetables until tender. Add chicken and cook until meat is done. Add salt and pepper, bouillon cube, and water. Continue cooking until cube dissolves. Add the croutons and stir into mixture until liquid is absorbed and croutons are soft. If you substitute Minute Rice for the croutons, cover the pot and let it sit off the heat for a few minutes. (Cooking time will vary depending on the stove and altitude.)

Here's a similar theme, but with a slightly different taste and look.

◑◑ POTTED CHICKEN

2 medium carrots, cut in chunks
½ stalk celery, sliced
1 small onion, sliced
2 medium potatoes, peeled and diced
2 chicken bouillon cubes
1 cup water
2 boneless, skinless chicken breasts
salt and pepper to taste
dried basil to taste

Place vegetables, bouillon, and water in pot. Bring to a boil over medium flame. Reduce heat and stir. Place chicken on top of veggies; season with salt, pepper, and basil. Cover and continue to cook over low flame for 30 minutes or until chicken is done. Add water as needed to keep broth level up.

The great thing about chicken is that it doesn't affect the flavor of the dish as strongly as red meats do. That lets you do some fun things with sauces and vegetables that might otherwise vanish in competition.

POWDERHORN CHICKEN

2 tablespoons butter or margarine
1 small onion, diced
½ tablespoon paprika
½ pound boneless chicken breast (or softpack), cubed
¾ cup water
½ teaspoon salt (optional)
pepper to taste
1 medium green pepper, diced
1 medium red pepper, diced
4 ounces cream cheese (use nonfat if you want)

Over medium flame, heat pot. Melt butter, add onions, and cook until browned. Add paprika and chicken and cook over low heat for about 20 minutes. Add water, salt and pepper, and remaining veggies. Cover and cook for another 15 to 20 minutes, stirring occasionally. Add cream cheese a lump at a time, letting each lump melt and mix into the sauce. Serve with chunks of sourdough or other hearty bread. This dish really goes well with pasta, which you can precook at home.

◗◗   HOT 'N' STEAMY CHICKEN

1 large carrot, peeled and sliced
1 large potato, peeled and sliced
1 medium green pepper, sliced into spears
1 medium onion, in chunks
1 tablespoon light brown sugar
salt, pepper, and curry powder to taste
2 chicken legs, disjointed
3 tablespoons water

Place vegetables in pot. Combine brown sugar, salt, pepper, and curry powder. Coat chicken with this mixture. Place chicken on top of vegetables. Add water and cover pot. Cook over medium flame about 40 minutes. Check to make sure water doesn't evaporate. Add liquid as needed to avoid burning. Scrape veggies away from bottom of pot if they begin to stick, but don't stir mixture.

○ CALCUTTA CHICKEN

2 teaspoons vegetable oil
1 medium onion, finely chopped
1 stalk celery, finely chopped
½ pound boneless, skinless chicken breast (or softpack), cut in 1-inch cubes
⅓ cup flour
2 chicken bouillon cubes dissolved in 1½ cups water
1 6-ounce can tomato juice
1 teaspoon curry powder
½ teaspoon Worcestershire sauce
precooked rice

Heat oil in pot over medium flame and sauté vegetables until tender. Add chicken and cook until done, stirring occasionally. Add flour and stir to mix. Add bouillon mixture immediately, and cook until sauce is smooth and thick. Add tomato juice, curry powder, and Worcestershire. Cover and simmer for 5 minutes. Serve over precooked rice.

BARCELONA BIRD

1 tablespoon olive oil
½ pound boneless, skinless chicken breast (or softpack), cut in 1-inch cubes
1 large tomato, cubed
1 medium green pepper, diced
1 medium onion, chopped
1 6-ounce can tomato paste
¾ cup water
¼ teaspoon cayenne pepper
salt and pepper to taste
¾ cup uncooked Minute Rice (optional)
¼ cup black olives, diced (optional)

Heat oil in pot over medium flame. Add chicken and cook for 10 minutes. Add veggies and sauté until chicken is tender. Add the remaining ingredients except rice and olives. Simmer sauce to very slow bubbling boil. Add rice and stir into mix. Cover and set aside for 5 minutes. Sprinkle with olives, if desired.

Keeping the international flavor, let's cross the Mediterranean and take a stroll on the Appian Way.

COLOSSAL CHICKEN

1 tablespoon olive oil
2 boneless chicken breasts (or softpack), cut in 1-inch chunks
1 medium onion, diced
1 clove garlic, crushed
3 large mushrooms, sliced
1 6-ounce can tomato paste
1 cup water
1 very ripe tomato, crushed
½ teaspoon oregano
¼ teaspoon each basil, black pepper, and fennel seed
1 teaspoon sugar
1 tablespoon grated Parmesan cheese
precooked spaghetti

Heat oil in pot over medium flame. Brown chicken, turning to prevent sticking. Add vegetables and sauté until tender. Add remaining ingredients except pasta. Stir until tomato paste is incorporated. Reduce heat, cover, and cook for about 30 minutes. Balance seasonings as you wish. Serve with precooked spaghetti.

Tip: For a powerful spaghetti sauce, try this without the chicken. Consider crumbling a bay leaf and dicing up green peppers to amplify the aroma and enhance the appearance.

Friends have asked me about the old Saturday night favorite, franks and beans. I've said many times that hot dogs are an easy way out of having to think when you're cooking. However, the beans are another story.

BOSTON BASTED BIRD

2 boneless, skinless chicken breasts
6 strips thick-cut bacon
1 12-ounce can baked beans, drained and repackaged
½ cup raisins
1 tablespoon brown sugar

Wrap 3 strips bacon around each chicken breast. Heat pot over medium flame and brown meat. Cook for about 10 minutes, turning to keep from burning. Drain excess grease. Combine baked beans, raisins, and brown sugar. Pour mixture over chicken and bacon, making sure the meat is well covered. Cover pot and simmer over low heat about 25 minutes. Serve with brown bread.

Tip: This can also be prepared as a casserole for the oven. Follow the recipe to the point of simmering over low heat. Instead, place it in oven pan, cover, and bake 1 hour at medium heat.

☉ CHICAGO-STYLE CHICKEN

4 tablespoons flour
1 tablespoon dry mustard
1 teaspoon pepper
2 boneless chicken breasts, cut in strips
1 tablespoon vegetable oil
1 medium onion, chopped
2 cups milk (fresh, or from powdered)
1 tomato, thinly sliced
1 tablespoon chopped fresh parsley
1 stalk celery, chopped
1 dill pickle, chopped (optional)

Combine 3 tablespoons flour, mustard, and pepper in plastic bag. Place chicken in bag and shake to coat. In pot, heat oil and brown chicken, turning to avoid burning. Add onion and sauté until tender. Add remaining tablespoon flour to milk and add to pot, heating to a boil (do not burn). Add tomato, parsley, and celery. Reduce heat, cover, and cook for 20 to 25 minutes or until chicken is done. Stir to prevent sticking. Serve with hard roll and garnish with a chopped dill pickle, if desired.

If you like mushrooms, you're sure to like this recipe.

☉☉ MUSHED CHICKEN

½ tablespoon vegetable oil
4 to 5 large mushrooms, sliced
1 medium onion, finely chopped
2 chicken bouillon cubes
1 cup water
2 boneless, skinless chicken breasts
oregano to taste
pepper to taste
1 cup uncooked Minute Rice
2 carrots, cut in thin curls

In pot over medium flame, heat oil and sauté mushrooms and onion. When vegetables are tender, add water and bouillon cubes. Bring to boil. Reduce heat and place chicken on top of vegetables. Season with oregano and pepper. Cover and cook for 35 minutes. Remove chicken and add rice. Stir to mix. Return chicken to pot. Drop carrots on top of all. Cover and cook another 5 minutes. Remove pot from stove and let sit 5 minutes before removing cover.

This next dish goes great over noodles or French bread.

�𝗨�𝗨 CHICKEN 'N' GREEN-EYED GRAVY

nonstick cooking spray
2 boneless chicken breasts (or softpack), cut in chunks
1 medium onion, chopped
3/4 cup water
1 chicken bouillon cube
3/4 cup freeze-dried peas
salt and pepper to taste
flour and water to thicken

Spray pot and heat over medium flame. Brown chicken, but do not burn. Add onion and cook until soft. Add all other ingredients except flour and cook for about 20 minutes or until peas are soft. Add additional water as needed. Thicken gravy by making a mix of water and flour and stirring in slowly to prevent lumps.

The search for flavor being the mother of invention, here's a quick and easy way to tickle your taste buds.

CREAMED CHICKEN AND NOODLES

2 chicken bouillon cubes
1½ cups water
2 boneless, skinless chicken breasts (or softpack), cut in chunks
4 ounces cream cheese (use nonfat if you want)
½ cup freeze-dried peas
2 tablespoons flour
1 red pepper, diced
1 cup precooked noodles or macaroni

In pot, bring bouillon cubes and water to boil. Add all other ingredients (add cream cheese a chunk at a time) except noodles. Reduce heat, cover, and simmer for 30 minutes. Stir occasionally. Serve over precooked noodles.

This next recipe is about as simple as you can get in a pot. You do, however, have to carry the bones out after enjoying this dish in the wild.

∪∪   OLD-FASHIONED CHICKEN FRICASSEE

4 chicken legs, disjointed
1½ cups water (approximate)
1 medium onion, sliced
2 carrots, peeled and sliced
1 tablespoon flour
1 cup nonfat milk (fresh, or from powdered)
salt and pepper to taste
precooked noodles or biscuits

Place chicken legs in pot and add enough water to cover. Once water boils, add onion and carrots. Cook over medium flame for 35 to 45 minutes or until meat begins coming off bones. (There should be at least 1 cup of liquid left in pot.) Mix milk and flour together and add to pot. Bring to boil, stirring gently to prevent sticking. Add salt and pepper as desired. Serve over precooked noodles or biscuits.

Don't think you have to put your pot over the flame to make a sumptuous meal. Try this one on for size.

TASTY CHICKEN SALAD

  3 tablespoons honey
  2 tablespoons vegetable oil
  juice of 1 lemon
  ½ teaspoon onion salt (optional)
  2 stalks celery, diced
  1 tablespoon Dijon mustard
  1 softpack chicken (about 7 ounces)
  1½ cups chop suey noodles

In pot, whisk together all ingredients except chicken and noodles. Add chicken and noodles and toss to coat with dressing.

Soups and Stews

When archaeologists examine the human record, they often evaluate civilizations based on the decorations found on potsherds turned up in the diggings. To me that says one thing: the ancients knew that the pot was more than just a water-gathering device. It was the center of the home; the symbol of the hearth that provided for all who clustered around.

  Over the years, soups and stews have been a mainstay in the wilderness menu. The ingredients are relatively easy to carry, since the heaviest is the one you dip out of a lake, and you can make a lot of soup quickly. I've found that the best time for a soup or stew is when the wind is cutting and I need warming up fast. Pouring a quart of water in the pot and tossing in a handful of vegetables, seasonings, and meat leaves me ample time to get a tent pitched and gear readied. Then it's time to eat!

For the Basic Soup recipe, you can combine all the dry ingredients in a bag at home. Then all you have to do is dump them into the boiling water without taking time to measure.

BASIC SOUP

   1 tablespoon oil (optional)
   ½ pound meat (optional)
   4 cups water
   4 chicken or beef bouillon cubes
   1 small tomato, 2 to 3 tablespoons tomato paste, or
       small handful of sun-dried tomatoes
   1 carrot, chopped (freeze-dried is OK)
   ½ cup freeze-dried peas
   ½ cup freeze-dried potato slices
   1 teaspoon celery seeds
   2 tablespoons dried parsley
   2 tablespoons dried onion flakes
   pepper to taste
   garlic powder to taste

In pot over medium flame, heat oil and brown meat. Do not burn. Add water and bouillon cubes. Bring to a boil and add all other ingredients. Reduce heat and cover. Simmer for about 25 to 30 minutes.

ʊʊ FAST PEA SOUP

3 cups water
¼ teaspoon salt (optional)
1 cup freeze-dried peas (more for thicker soup)
½ cup lean ham, diced
2 carrots, diced
1 teaspoon thyme

In pot over medium flame, bring salted water to boil. Add all ingredients and cover. Simmer for about 45 minutes or longer to cook down peas, stirring occasionally. Serve with soda crackers or bread.

This next soup was inspired by those hardy souls who paddled the North Country in search of furs during the 18th and 19th centuries. It takes a long time to cook, so keep it for a layover day on your trip.

ʊʊ VOYAGEUR PEA SOUP

4 cups water (or more)
2 cups dried (not freeze-dried) yellow or green peas
salt and pepper to taste
½ cup ham, diced
1 large onion, diced
1 large carrot, peeled and diced
1 to 2 tablespoons flour

Soak dried peas in water for about 6 hours. (I use my 32-ounce Nalgene bottle and load peas and water in the a.m. for soup in the p.m.) When ready to cook, add water to bring to 2 cups. Add salt and pepper and bring to boil over medium flame, stirring to prevent sticking. Add ham, onion, and carrot. Cover and reduce heat. Cook for at least 1 hour, adding water as needed or flour to thicken if desired.

Sometimes, familiar territory tastes best when your stomach asks if the soup's on.

DON'S PENICILLIN

   5 cups water
   1 teaspoon salt (optional)
   2 chicken legs, disjointed
   4 carrots, peeled and diced
   2 tablespoons onion flakes
   pepper to taste
   2 bay leaves
   ¼ teaspoon thyme
   1 cup uncooked noodles

In pot over medium flame, bring salted water to gentle boil. Cook chicken until meat falls off bone (about 45 minutes), adding water as needed. Remove meat and bones from broth. Discard bones and cut meat into small pieces. Add all other ingredients except noodles. Cook another 25 minutes or until carrots are done. Add noodles and cook until tender.

The powers of chicken soup are legendary. Yet for me, the ultimate chicken soup has to be a major meal in a bowl. And that means chicken stew.

◡◡ SOUPER CLUCK STEW

   1 softpack chicken, cut in chunks
   4 cups water (or more)
   4 chicken bouillon cubes
   4 potatoes, peeled and diced
   2 medium carrots, chopped
   2 medium onions, chopped
   ½ teaspoon cayenne pepper
   2 cloves garlic, crushed
   ½ teaspoon pepper
   1 large tomato, cut in chunks
   1 cup dried corn
   flour (optional)

Place all ingredients except corn and tomato in pot over medium to high flame. Bring to boil, cover, and reduce heat. Simmer 30 minutes. Add corn and tomato, and simmer another 15 minutes. Add water as needed. Thicken with flour if needed.

ʊʊ CHOW-HOUND CHOWDER

1 softpack chicken
3 cups water
½ cup freeze-dried corn
½ cup onion flakes
2 stalks celery, chopped
1 packet dried nonfat milk (1-quart size, or 1⅓ cups)
salt and pepper to taste
2 to 3 tablespoons flour

In pot, mix all ingredients except flour. Heat over medium flame until corn is rehydrated. If thickening is needed, mix flour with a few tablespoons of water to make a paste. Stir well while adding this to stew to prevent lumps.

You might just want to be a little corny, too.

◊ CORN CHOWDER

1 tablespoon vegetable oil
1 medium onion, diced
1 stalk celery, diced
2 tablespoons flour
1 cup water
½ cup freeze-dried corn
½ cup low-fat milk (or make from powdered)
salt and pepper to taste

Heat oil in pot over medium flame. Add the diced vegetables. Sauté for 2 to 3 minutes. Add the flour and cook (don't let veggies or flour brown!) for another 4 minutes. Add the water, corn, and milk. Bring to a boil over high flame and cook, stirring occasionally. Season with salt and pepper, reduce heat to a low simmer, and cook for another 10 minutes. Add water as needed to achieve desired thickness.

Instead of "cluck," you might want "moo" in your meal. If so, take a shot at a high-powered soup that's got more mulligan in it than a 6:45 a.m. Saturday tee time.

BIG-TIME BEEF STEW

½ pound stew beef, cut in 1-inch cubes
1 cup flour
2 to 3 tablespoons vegetable oil
2 cups water
2 medium potatoes, cubed (leave peel on)
1 medium onion, cut in chunks
2 carrots, cut in chunks
salt and pepper to taste
1 bay leaf
1 teaspoon Worcestershire sauce
celery seed to taste
1 egg, beaten

Place flour in bowl and dredge meat in flour. Over medium flame, heat pot and add oil. Brown floured meat, turning to prevent sticking. Save leftover flour. Add water to pot, scraping bottom with spoon. Add all other ingredients except egg, cover, and simmer at least 30 minutes. Stir occasionally. Add a little water, a few dashes of vegetable oil, and the beaten egg to remaining flour. Mix into a sticky dough. With oiled spoon, drop balls of dough into stew, cover pot again, and cook 5 minutes more. *Do not stir* stew after you add the dumplings.

This is a hearty soup that uses a beef soup bone and ham hocks. If you're not going to be at a campsite with access to a garbage can, you may want to try a different soup recipe or you'll end up lugging some heavy waste around with you.

LONG DAY SOUP

- 1 beef soup bone
- 2 ham hocks (about 1½ pounds)
- 1 teaspoon cayenne pepper
- 2 cups black-eyed peas (presoak 4 to 5 hours in 2 quarts of cold water)
- 2 large onions, cut in chunks
- 1 gallon water

Boil all ingredients over medium to medium-high heat for 1 hour until peas are soft. Strip meat from beef bone and ham hocks and reserve. Discard fat, skin, and bones. Remove ½ cup of peas from soup and mash with fork. Mix mashed peas into broth. Return meat to soup and simmer for another 30 minutes.

Here's a vegetarian stew from my friend Chris
Townsend.

ʊʊ   CARROT AND LENTIL STEW

4 cups water
½ cup lentils
2 large carrots, diced
1 large onion, diced
2 garlic cloves, crushed
1 large tomato, cut in chunks
¼ cup fresh parsley, chopped
2 bay leaves
black pepper to taste
chili powder to taste (optional)
pinch of salt

Add all ingredients except salt to water (use more water
if you prefer a soupy stew), bring to a boil, and then simmer 45 minutes or until lentils are soft. Add salt after
cooking (adding it before slows down cooking). Cooking
time can be shortened if lentils are presoaked in hot
water. Serve with whole-grain bread.

Vegetables

And speaking of vegetarian dishes, here are a few recipes
to make your trail meals greener and tastier. For a hearty
vegetarian pasta dish, try Pasta and Sauce (see page 119)
without the beef. Get some extra fiber and even more tex-
ture by using whole wheat pasta. For a powerful ratatouille, try the recipe on page 117, substituting mushrooms
for the meat. And for other vegetable dishes, turn to the
vegetable section in the previous chapter (see pages 64–69)
and treat your pot like a pan.

VERY GREEN STUFFED PEPPERS

1 large onion, half diced and half sliced ¼ inch thick
1 cup precooked wild rice
¾ cup precooked Minute Rice
1 large tomato, diced
½ cup seasoned breadcrumbs
1 egg, beaten
6 ounces cheddar cheese (use reduced fat if you want), grated
¼ cup green olives stuffed with pimentos, chopped
salt and pepper to taste
2 large green peppers
½ to ¾ cup water

In bowl, mix all ingredients except onion slices, peppers, and water. Cut tops off green peppers and clean out seeds. Stuff peppers. Place onion slices on bottom of pot. Place peppers on top of onions. Add water and cover. Over a medium flame, bring water to a boil and cook peppers 45 minutes.

The next recipe can work either as a complement to a meal or as a quick stand-alone lunch.

TASTY PASTA WITH CHEESE

2 to 3 quarts water
2 teaspoons salt
1 cup uncooked pasta
2 tablespoons olive oil
2 teaspoons vegetable oil
¼ teaspoon hot pepper flakes
salt and pepper to taste
½ cup shelled walnut pieces or pine nuts
½ cup grated cheese (use reduced fat if you want)

Boil salted water in your pot. Add pasta and cook until done. Drain water. Add all other ingredients and toss gently to coat.

SPAGHETTI WITH CHEESE AND TOMATO SAUCE

2 to 3 quarts water
8 ounces uncooked spaghetti or noodles
1 large onion, sliced
1 15-ounce can whole or diced tomatoes, undrained
grated Parmesan or other hard cheese, as much as you
    like!
1 garlic clove, crushed
1 tablespoon mixed herbs (such as oregano, basil, and
    fennel seed)
black pepper to taste

Boil water in your pot. Add spaghetti and onion, and
cook uncovered for 10 minutes or until spaghetti is
cooked, stirring occasionally. Drain water. Add tomatoes,
cheese, garlic, and herbs and return to heat, stirring constantly until cheese has melted.

◡◡ "IT'S ALL WE HAD IN THE DEPRESSION" TOMATO LUNCH

2¼ cups water
3 large tomatoes
1 green pepper, diced
1 onion, diced
2 tablespoons sugar
salt and pepper to taste
½ cup uncooked Minute Rice

In pot, bring 2 cups water to boil. Scald tomatoes by dip-
ping them in water with slotted spoon for 30 seconds to
1 minute. Remove from water and peel. Discard water.
Return tomatoes to pot and add remaining ¼ cup water.
Cover and cook over low flame for 20 minutes. Add all
other ingredients and cook another 10 to 15 minutes, stirring to prevent sticking.

RIB-STICKIN' POTATO SALAD

    water
    3 large potatoes, peeled and quartered
    2 eggs
    ¼ cup green onion, diced
    3 to 4 tablespoons Miracle Whip or mayonnaise
    1 tablespoon prepared mustard
    salt and pepper to taste
    1 cup mushrooms, sliced (optional)

Place potatoes and eggs in pot and add enough water to cover. Boil for 25 minutes. Drain and cut potatoes into small chunks. Peel and dice eggs. Mix with all remaining ingredients in pot. For still more protein, add mushrooms.

Here's another from Chris Townsend.

RICE CURRY

    1 tablespoon vegetable oil
    1 cup brown rice
    1 large onion, sliced
    ½ teaspoon curry powder (or to taste)
    2 cups water
    1 cup mushrooms, sliced
    ½ cup raisins
    1 large green pepper, chopped
    1 large tomato, chopped
    1 vegetable bouillon cube

In pot over medium flame, heat oil. Add rice, onion, and curry powder and sauté 1 minute, stirring constantly. Then add the rest of the ingredients. Bring to boil and then simmer, covered, until all the water has been absorbed (about 30 minutes). You can use white rice instead of brown; it cooks in half the time but the result won't be as tasty or nutritious.

Here's an unusual dish that makes a great cold lunch. Top it off with fruit.

CHILLED SESAME LINGUINE

2 to 3 quarts water
½ pound thin linguine or spaghetti
1 tablespoon peanut oil
1 teaspoon minced fresh ginger
4 teaspoons sugar
2 tablespoons creamy peanut butter
2 tablespoons soy sauce
1 tablespoon wine vinegar
¼ teaspoon crushed red pepper flakes
2 scallions, cut into 2-inch pieces

Boil water in large pot and cook pasta. Drain and toss with peanut oil; set aside to cool. In small bowl, whisk together remaining ingredients except scallions. Pour over cooled pasta. Before serving, toss well and sprinkle scallions over the top.

One of our favorite recipes is something my wife, Pam, picked up while she was taking a course at Northern Illinois University.

◑◑ VEGETARIAN CHILI

1 cup Textured Vegetable Protein (TVP); available at
    many natural food stores
⅞ cup boiling water
1 medium onion, chopped
1 teaspoon olive oil
1 14½-ounce can whole tomatoes, undrained
1 15-ounce can kidney beans, drained
1 to 2 cups vegetable broth
1 tablespoon chili powder
1 teaspoon dried oregano
½ teaspoon cumin powder
salt to taste

In small bowl, combine boiling water and TVP to rehydrate (takes about 10 minutes). In a heavy pot, sauté onion in oil. Add all the remaining ingredients. Reserve 1 cup of broth, adding as necessary to achieve desired thickness. Simmer uncovered for 15 minutes, stirring occasionally. Serves 4.

The next recipe is a salute to Jill Seals, Kern River kayaker.

ᴗᴗ SEALS SALAD

- ½ cup precooked brown rice
- ½ cup precooked white rice
- 1 green onion, chopped
- 2 radishes, chopped
- ½ cup canned or fresh bean sprouts, rinsed, drained, and chopped
- 1 medium green pepper, diced
- 5 small black olives, pitted and diced
- 1 small Roma tomato, seeded and diced
- ⅓ cup grated cheddar cheese (use reduced fat if you want)
- 3 tablespoons balsamic vinegar
- ½ teaspoon Mrs. Dash seasoning

Mix all ingredients in pot except vinegar and Mrs. Dash seasoning. In a cup, mix the vinegar and Mrs. Dash seasoning. Pour dressing over salad and toss until coated.

Tip: For an even lower-fat salad, use nonfat cheese. For a taste variation (but also an increase in fat), substitute chop suey noodles for the sprouts.

Meat

Your pot gives you a chance to experiment with beef in ways you just can't do in a frying pan. The simple fact is that, depending on the cut, beef can be tough and stringy. Cheap cuts cooked in a frying pan can mean tough times when the dinner bell rings.

The pot helps solve that problem. Because you'll be cooking the meat for more than 30 minutes in most cases, you can use chuck or round where you might otherwise want sirloin. The extended cooking will help tenderize the cheaper cuts, which means you can go easy on your purse while building a meal that goes easy on your taste buds.

Beef has a stronger flavor than poultry and supports more heady spice combinations. Don't be afraid to experiment. Beef also makes a heartier gravy that presents well against starches such as potatoes, noodles, and rice.

BASIC BEEF IN A POT

½ pound boneless bottom round, cut in strips
3 tablespoons flour
2 tablespoons vegetable oil

Choose one of the following sauces:

Red Sauce
1 green pepper, diced
½ cup water
1 large tomato, crushed
1 teaspoon onion flakes
¼ teaspoon paprika
salt and pepper to taste

Cream Sauce
3 large mushrooms, sliced
1 medium potato, thinly sliced
1 cup water mixed with ⅔ cup powdered milk, or 1 cup
    nonfat milk
1 tablespoon flour
pepper to taste

Brown Sauce
1 carrot, chopped
1 tablespoon sugar
1 cup water
1 tablespoon flour
1 teaspoon onion flakes
¼ teaspoon garlic powder
salt and pepper to taste

In a plastic bag, shake beef in flour until coated. In pot over medium flame, heat oil and brown meat, taking care not to burn meat. For the Red Sauce, add green pepper and sauté until tender, adding extra oil if needed. For the Cream Sauce variation, sauté mushrooms and potato. For the Brown Sauce recipe, sauté carrot and add sugar to caramelize both the vegetable and the beef.

At this point, add all other ingredients for the selected sauce base. Reduce heat and cover. Cook between 35 and 45 minutes, stirring occasionally to prevent sticking. Add water to keep sauce reduction to a minimum. Serve over noodles, over rice, or with rolls. If you didn't bring pre-cooked noodles or rice, you can add either one to the pot before the final 35- to 45-minute simmering. Just be sure you have enough liquid left to cook the starch—add more if necessary. An uncooked vegetable as a side dish will fill out the meal.

No doubt you've figured out that the pot, like the frying pan, is a great way to take a trip around the world. Sort of like taking one trek and then adding another to it.

GARIBALDI'S ROAST BEEF

  ½ to ¾ pound rump or round roast
  2 teaspoons olive oil
  ½ teaspoon garlic powder
  ½ teaspoon basil
  2 tablespoons prepared mustard
  2 tablespoons olive oil
  1 cup water
  1 medium green pepper, cut in strips
  2 medium potatoes, sliced (leave peel on)
  1 medium red pepper, cut in strips
  1 large onion, chopped

Rub oil, garlic powder, basil, and mustard on roast. Heat oil in pot over medium flame. Brown meat on all sides. Add water, cover, and cook about 1 hour. Add vegetables. Cover and cook another 30 minutes. Serve with Italian bread.

⊖⊖ PEDRO'S RICE

  ½ pound ground beef (95 percent lean)
  1 large onion, chopped
  1 medium green pepper, chopped
  5 plum tomatoes, crushed
  1½ cups water
  ¾ cup uncooked rice
  ½ teaspoon chili powder
  salt and pepper to taste

In pot over medium flame, brown meat until crumbly and drain grease. Add all other ingredients and stir thoroughly. Bring to moderate boil. Cover, reduce heat, and cook about 20 minutes or until rice is tender.

Normally, the following recipe uses only vegetables. I've found that beef makes an interesting taste difference, however. If you want to make it vegetarian, substitute 2 cups of sliced portobello mushrooms for the meat.

BEEF RATATOUILLE

3 tablespoons olive oil
½ pound round steak, thinly sliced
1 large onion, sliced
1 clove garlic, crushed
1 large green pepper, diced
1 medium to large summer squash or zucchini, sliced
1 medium eggplant, diced
1 large tomato, cut in chunks
1 6-ounce can tomato paste
1 cup water
2 to 3 tablespoons sugar
1 bay leaf
¼ teaspoon fennel seed
salt and pepper to taste
grated Parmesan or Romano cheese (optional)

Heat oil in pot over medium flame. Brown meat, add onion, and sauté until onion is soft. Add all other ingredients. Cover and reduce heat. Stir often. Cook about 35 minutes or until sauce thickens. Sprinkle with Parmesan or Romano cheese.

◊ "SAFE" CHILI

½ to ¾ pound sirloin, cut in bite-size chunks
1 teaspoon vegetable oil
1 large onion, chopped
1 clove garlic, crushed
1 large tomato, chopped
6 large mushrooms, sliced
½ cup freeze-dried corn
1 6-ounce can tomato paste
¾ cup water
1½ teaspoons chili powder
¼ teaspoon pepper
¼ teaspoon ground cumin
salt to taste

In pot over medium flame, heat oil and brown meat. Add all other ingredients. Cover and simmer for 15 to 20 minutes or until vegetables are tender.

Here is another version of an old-time favorite.

MEATY STUFFED PEPPERS

½ to ¾ pound ground beef (95 percent lean)
1 large onion, half diced and half sliced ¼ inch thick
⅔ cup uncooked Minute Rice
1 medium tomato, diced
1 egg, beaten
¼ teaspoon hot pepper sauce
garlic salt and pepper to taste
2 large green peppers
½ cup water

In bowl, mix all ingredients except onion slices, peppers, and water. Cut tops off green peppers and remove seeds. Divide stuffing evenly and pack each pepper. Place onion slices on bottom of pot. Place peppers upright in pot on top of onion slices, add water, and cover. Over medium flame, bring water to boil. Cook 45 minutes. Check to keep water level at least 1 inch up on peppers.

Sticking with good ground beef for a moment, here's another old-time favorite that's super easy when you're toting a pot.

PASTA AND SAUCE

½ to ¾ pound ground beef (95 percent lean)
1 tablespoon olive oil
1 medium onion, diced
1 clove garlic, crushed
1 medium green pepper, diced
1 large tomato, crushed
1 6-ounce can tomato paste
1 cup water
2 teaspoons oregano
1 teaspoon basil
½ teaspoon fennel seed
1½ tablespoons sugar
2 tablespoons grated Parmesan cheese
salt and pepper to taste
2 cups precooked pasta

In pot over low flame, brown ground beef. Drain and add oil. Heat over medium flame. Add onion, garlic, and green pepper and sauté with meat until tender. Add tomato paste, water, seasonings, sugar, and cheese, stirring to mix evenly. Simmer 25 minutes. Add salt and pepper to taste, then mix in precooked pasta. Add water if blend becomes too dry. Remove from heat and serve with Caesar salad. For a vegetarian sauce, omit the meat.

BEEFY, CHEESY ELBOWS

2 teaspoons vegetable oil
⅔ pound ground beef (95 percent lean)
1 large onion, diced
4 ounces cheddar cheese (use reduced fat if you want),
    cubed
½ cup milk
salt and pepper to taste
4 cups precooked macaroni

Heat pot over medium flame and add oil. Sauté beef and onion until well cooked. Spoon off as much grease as possible. Add cheese, milk, and seasonings. Cover and simmer over low heat until cheese is melted. Add macaroni. Heat for 5 minutes and serve.

A traditional pot recipe comes to us from the farms and chateaus of France.

DRUNKEN BEEF

¾ pound sirloin, cut in 1-inch chunks
flour
2 tablespoon oil, butter, or margarine
1 large onion, chopped
1 clove garlic, diced
1 package mushroom soup (single-serving size)
1 cup water
salt and pepper to taste
½ cup dry red wine
2 cups precooked noodles

Dredge meat in flour. Heat oil in pot over medium flame. Brown the beef. Add onion and garlic and sauté until tender. Add all other ingredients. Bring to boil. Reduce heat, cover, and simmer 35 minutes. Serve over precooked noodles.

Other traditions can be found closer to home. You might want to bring a 2-quart pot if this is going to be Saturday night dinner.

ʘ CORNED BEEF À LA MICHAEL

¾ pound lean corned beef, well trimmed and rinsed
water
½ head cabbage
2 large onions, quartered
2 large potatoes, peeled and cut in half
4 carrots, cut in chunks
1 teaspoon celery flakes
2 bay leaves
pepper to taste

In pot, cover meat with water and simmer about 1 hour, making sure that water does not boil off. Drain water and add all other ingredients. Cover meat and vegetables with fresh water. Bring to gentle boil, reduce heat, and cover. Cook over low flame about 1 hour.

ʘʘ TICK-TOCK MINUTE STEAK

2 cube steaks (about ½ pound total)
salt and pepper to taste
garlic powder to taste
1 large onion, sliced
1 cup uncooked Minute Rice
1 cup fresh green beans, chopped
1 6-ounce can tomato paste
2 cups water

Season meat with salt, pepper, and garlic powder. Layer ingredients in pot: onion, then meat, then rice, then beans. Combine water and tomato paste and pour over everything. Cover and cook over medium heat 30 minutes.

BEEF À LA MACARTHUR

¼ pound dried beef (4-ounce jar or bag)
1 cup water
1 cup milk (fresh, or from powdered)
2 to 3 tablespoons flour
2 hard-boiled eggs, chopped
salt and pepper to taste

In pot over medium flame, bring meat and water to boil. Cook about 5 minutes. Remove from heat and drain water. This helps reduce the saltiness. Add milk and return to heat. Warm, but *do not boil.* Slowly stir in flour to thicken sauce. Add eggs and season with salt and pepper. Cook no longer than 5 minutes more. Serve over a split hard roll. Serves 1.

The crowning achievement for beef in a pot is just that—the all-American pot roast.

ᴓᴓ   RED, WHITE, AND BROWN POT ROAST

½ to ¾ pound pot roast (boneless, if possible)
salt and pepper to taste
nonstick cooking spray
2 cups water
3 beef bouillon cubes
2 large potatoes, peeled and quartered
3 large carrots, sliced
1 or 2 large onions, cut in chunks

Season meat with salt and pepper. Spray pot and heat over medium flame. Add meat and brown quickly on all sides. Immediately add remaining ingredients and simmer over medium flame 45 minutes or longer. Stir occasionally to keep from sticking.

Beyond beef are pork and ham. All too often I've heard the complaint that pork is too dry. In the pot, it won't be.

◑◑ PEASANT PORK CHOPS

2 stalks celery, chopped
1 medium onion, cut in chunks
2 carrots, cut in chunks
1 large potato, quartered
1 large tomato, crushed
1 medium turnip, peeled and cut in chunks
½ teaspoon salt (optional)
1 beef bouillon cube
1 bay leaf
¼ teaspoon thyme
pepper to taste
1½ cups water
2 center-cut pork loin chops (trimmed of fat)

Combine all vegetables and seasonings with water in pot. Place chops on top. Cover and cook over a medium flame for 1 hour. Stir once after 30 minutes. Make sure that water does not boil away.

SOUPER CHOPS

2 center-cut pork loin chops, thick cut
⅔ cup uncooked Minute Rice
2 cups water
1 can mushroom soup (condensed is best)
1 single-serving packet onion soup mix
½ pound baby carrots

Combine all ingredients in pot, mix well, cover, and bring to boil. Stir to keep rice from sticking, reduce heat, and cook over low heat for 30 minutes. Stir occasionally to prevent burning.

○ BIG MO CHOPS

2 center-cut pork loin chops, thick cut (about 6 ounces
   each, and trimmed of fat)
1 large onion, sliced
1 large green pepper, cut in strips
2 large potatoes, sliced
2 tablespoons ketchup
2 tablespoons molasses
2 tablespoons water

In pot over medium flame, brown chops. Remove from pot and drain fat. Layer ingredients as follows: sliced onion, then meat, then other vegetables. Brush with ketchup and molasses. Drizzle water over top. Cover and cook 40 minutes over low heat. Add additional water if sauce is too thick.

And what about bacon? It isn't just for breakfast anymore.

BELLY BUSTIN' SPUDS

½ pound bacon, diced
1 large onion, chopped
1 large green pepper, chopped
2 stalks celery, chopped
2 large potatoes, sliced (we're talking big bakers here!)
¼ cup fresh parsley, chopped

In pot over medium flame, cook bacon. Do not drain. Add onion, green pepper, and celery. Sauté until tender. Add potatoes, stir, and reduce heat. Stir occasionally. After 30 minutes, add parsley. Cook until potatoes start to fall apart.

DESSERT

Compotes, puddings, baked fruits—all are taste delights sure to top off a great meal. Your pot is the perfect venue for flavor and fun.

This unusual combination tastes great after a long day.

ʊʊ MAC'S SURPRISE

½ cup uncooked white rice
1 cup water
½ cup raisins
1 apple, peeled, cored, and sliced
1 tablespoon brown sugar
½ teaspoon cinnamon
¼ teaspoon nutmeg
1 tablespoon powdered nonfat milk

In pot over medium flame, combine rice and water and bring to boil. Add raisins and apple. Stir. Cover and cook until rice is tender, about 15 minutes. Remove from flame and add all other ingredients. Stir and let cool for 10 minutes. If you wish, add a little more milk and sugar.

INDIAN PUDDING

1 can sweetened condensed milk
½ cup water
3 tablespoons butter or margarine
3 tablespoons brown sugar
½ teaspoon nutmeg
½ teaspoon cinnamon
2 eggs, beaten
½ to ¾ cup cornmeal
¼ cup raisins

In pot over medium flame, bring sweetened condensed milk and water to gentle boil. Reduce heat and add butter, sugar, and spices. Once sugar is dissolved, add eggs, cornmeal, and raisins. Stir. Cover and cook over low flame for 10 minutes. Stir often to keep from sticking.

○○ ORANGE PUDDING

2 oranges, peeled and segmented (or substitute a
     6-ounce can of mandarin orange segments, drained)
1 teaspoon plus 1½ tablespoons sugar
⅔ cup milk (fresh, or from powdered)
1 egg yolk (reserve egg white for topping)
salt (optional)
2 teaspoons cornstarch

Topping
1 egg white
½ teaspoon sugar

For pudding, sprinkle 1 teaspoon sugar over oranges in
bowl. In pot over medium flame, combine milk, egg yolk,
a pinch of salt, cornstarch, and 1½ tablespoons sugar. Stir
until mixture thickens. Pour over oranges. Allow to cool. If
you wish a topping, whip egg white until stiff, fold in
sugar, and spoon onto pudding.

Here's a favorite of a British friend of mine.

TRIFLE

¾ cup fresh strawberries, sliced (or use blueberries)
sugar
2 Twinkies, sliced the long way

Custard
1 cup milk
2 egg yolks, beaten (reserve egg whites for topping)
2 tablespoons sugar
1 teaspoon cornstarch

Topping
2 egg whites
1 teaspoon sugar

Put berries in a bowl, sprinkle with sugar, and place the Twinkies on top. To make custard, combine milk, egg yolks, sugar, and cornstarch in a double boiler or pot over medium flame. Stir until mixture thickens. Pour over fruit and Twinkies. Allow to cool. If you wish a topping, beat egg whites until stiff, fold in sugar, and spoon onto trifle.

Earlier, we talked about steamed vegetables. Well, you can do the same with fruit.

ʊʊ APPLE DELIGHT

2 McIntosh apples, top halves peeled
2 tablespoons raisins
1 tablespoon sugar
cinnamon to taste
water

Core apples without puncturing bottoms. In bowl, mix sugar and raisins. Stuff each apple with raisin-sugar mixture. Sprinkle cinnamon over top. Pour enough water in pot to reach bottom of steamer. Place apples on steamer. Cover pot and place over medium flame. Allow to steam at least 30 minutes, adding water if needed.

ʊʊ PEARS 'N' COTS

Same recipe as previous, except substitute fresh pears for apples, diced dried apricots for raisins, and fresh mint leaves (finely diced) for cinnamon.

Creativity is the rule for desserts in a pot. You can stew or cook just about any fruit to make applesauce, "pearsauce," or fruit compote quickly and easily. Just chop the basic ingredients, add various spices to taste, and throw in molasses, brown sugar, or white sugar, depending on how you want the dish to look and taste.

♘♘ DON'S FRUIT COMPOTE

½ cup dried apricots
½ cup raisins
1 6-ounce can mandarin orange slices, drained
3 tablespoons sugar
⅓ cup water

In pot over medium flame, combine all ingredients. Cover and cook at least 20 minutes. Stir often and add more water as needed. Sauce should be thick. Serve with sponge cake or fancy cookies.

♘♘ SPICED APPLESAUCE

3 Granny Smith apples, peeled, cored, and cut in chunks
½ cup water
2 tablespoons brown sugar
½ teaspoon cinnamon
¼ teaspoon nutmeg

In pot over medium flame, cook apples in water until they fall apart. Remove from heat and stir to make sauce. Add sugar and spices. Tastes great with oatmeal cookies, or serve with or over oatmeal for breakfast!

THE OVEN

As Monty Python would say, "And now for something completely different." For a trekker, the height of adventurous cooking can be found in the outdoor oven. That's right, by simply firing up your stove you can operate an open-air kitchen that will challenge your culinary skills and your taste buds.

The Portable Kitchen chapter discussed ovens, both homemade and store bought. Both work equally well, and both produce casseroles, roasts, and baked treats in good order. And both keep you on your toes, making sure what you're cooking gets roasted to a turn, not burned to a crisp.

There are two differences between my homemade oven and a commercial product such as the Outback Oven. First, the coffee-can oven mimics a true oven in that the can is the body of the oven. That means you can cook items such as baked potatoes on the racks inside. The Outback Oven uses a pan-and-lid configuration inside a heat-capturing tent. The tent is the body of the oven, and the pan and lid make a sort of baking vessel. It's hard to cook a baked potato or a soufflé in it.

The other difference is that the Outback Oven is short—about 3 inches from bottom of pan to top of lid. That makes it difficult to cook upright dishes such as stuffed peppers. This oven is great, however, for pizza, biscuits, and combination dishes such as Uncle Ben's Chicken (see page 135). And if you're careful, you can use the bottom pan of this oven as a frying pan.

The recipes in this chapter will work equally well in any sort of backpacking oven. Also, unless otherwise indicated, all cooking temperatures should be in a "medium" oven of 325 to 350°F, or in the middle of the Bake scale on the Outback Oven's thermometer.

Remember that recipes with fewer than 30 percent fat calories are marked with a **◑**; those with fewer than 20 percent fat calories are marked with a **◑◑**.

BREAKFAST

Breakfast from the oven is a bit un-American because the national tendency is to eat breakfast cooked on the top of the stove. But there are some very satisfying ways to kick off the morning using your oven.

I'm an egg person, so I go for the yolk rather than the straight line. Remember that if you wish, you can replace beaten eggs in any recipe with a nonfat egg product like Egg Beaters. Simply freeze the unopened container and load it into your pack. Once thawed, you are ready to cook!

FRANÇOISE'S QUICHE

  1 prepared pie crust
  ½ cup cheddar cheese (use reduced fat if you want), diced
  ½ cup ham, diced
  ½ cup evaporated milk
  4 eggs
  salt and pepper to taste

Line a small oven pan with pie crust and cut off excess. Spread cheese on bottom and add ham on top of cheese. Beat milk, eggs, salt, and pepper together and pour over ham and cheese. In a medium oven (on lower rack) cook for 15 to 20 minutes or until filling is firm and top is browned.

ONIONY QUICHE

Same as previous recipe, but substitute sliced Bermuda onions for ham and use either Swiss or jack cheese (use reduced fat if you want).

(DON'T) BERN TH' EGGS!

1 tablespoon butter or margarine
⅓ cup Swiss cheese (use reduced fat if you want), grated
2 eggs
¼ cup evaporated milk

Warm oven pan over stove and melt butter. Sprinkle about three-quarters of the cheese on bottom of pan. Break eggs onto the cheese without breaking yolks. Pour milk over and sprinkle with remaining cheese. Place in medium oven 20 minutes. Serve with hard roll and fresh fruit. Serves 1.

McINTOSH GOBBLE

2 medium McIntosh apples
⅓ pound sausage (use turkey or soy if you want)
2 eggs
salt and pepper to taste

Core apples from the top, but don't break through bottom. Using a spoon, hollow out inside of apple to make a little pocket, widening opening at top. Fill about two-thirds full with sausage. Place in oven pan. Break an egg on top of the sausage (sides of apple will hold it in place). Bake in medium oven at least 25 to 30 minutes. Add salt and pepper to taste.

Note: When using an Outback Oven, you may have to trim the top of the apples to fit.

Your eyes will remember this recipe immediately. The
odor of onions on your hands will remind you of it all day.

BERMUDA EGGS

> 1 medium Bermuda onion
> 2 large eggs
> 1 tablespoon grated Parmesan cheese
> ¼ teaspoon tarragon
> 2 tablespoons fresh parsley, chopped
> 2 tablespoons breadcrumbs
> pepper to taste

Cut onion in half along "equator" (stem and root ends
being the poles). Scoop out inner rings of onion, leaving
two "cups." Place onion halves in oven pan and break an
egg into each. Dice remaining onion and sprinkle on eggs.
Combine cheese, tarragon, parsley, breadcrumbs, and pepper. Place healthy scoop on top of each onion. Gently
smooth to cover. Add extra as needed. Cook in medium
oven for about 15 minutes or until breadcrumbs are
browned. For added flavor, sprinkle with diced ham
before cooking. Serves 1 (if you're a 2-egger) or 2.

You can also use your oven to build some truly remark-
able creations.

AMSTERDAM APPLE PANCAKE

> 2 tablespoons butter or margarine
> 4 tablespoons brown sugar
> 2 large apples, peeled, cored, and sliced lengthwise
>   about ¼ inch thick
> ½ teaspoon cinnamon
> 2 eggs, beaten
> ½ cup milk
> ⅔ cup Bisquick

In oven pan, melt butter and spread brown sugar evenly on bottom of pan. Layer apple slices on sugar. Sprinkle with cinnamon. Combine egg, milk, and Bisquick and pour batter over fruit and sugar. Bake about 20 minutes in medium oven or until top of pancake is nicely browned. Flip onto plate so brown sugar and apples are on top.

RASHER CAKE

2 eggs, separated
½ cup milk
½ teaspoon sugar
½ cup flour
½ cup white cornmeal
1 teaspoon baking powder
pepper to taste
6 strips bacon (or use slices of Canadian bacon)

Beat egg yolks until light. Add remaining ingredients except bacon and egg whites. Beat egg whites until stiff. Fold into batter. Fry bacon in pan unil crisp and drain grease. Transfer bacon to oven pan, pour batter over, and bake in hot (400°F) oven 10 minutes. Reduce heat to medium (325°F) and continue baking until cake is set in center.

LUNCH AND DINNER

The oven offers countless opportunities to put variety into your menu from roasts, cakes, and casseroles to pies, bread, snacks, and even pizza. As far as I'm concerned, the oven is the best thing going when it's dinnertime.

Poultry

Chicken is one of the easiest meats to cook in the oven, but it can also be one of the most boring. So we'll start with the basics and spice it up from there.

Note: As mentioned before, two chicken breasts really mean one whole breast (which looks something like a valentine heart), cut in half. Each piece weighs 4 to 6 ounces.

◑ BBC (BASIC BAKED CHICKEN)

½ pound chicken (white or dark pieces) with skin
1 large onion, sliced
1 stalk celery, chopped
2 or 3 carrots, cut in strips
2 medium potatoes, cut in chunks
salt and pepper to taste

Place chicken in oven pan and surround with vegetables. Add salt and pepper. Bake about 45 minutes in medium oven. Remove skin before serving if you want. Serve with a hard roll and fruit.

'CUED BIRD

½ cup hot water
1 beef bouillon cube
1 fresh tomato, crushed
1 tablespoon Worcestershire sauce
4 tablespoons ketchup
1 onion, diced
¼ teaspoon dry mustard
1 teaspoon minced fresh parsley
¼ teaspoon salt (optional)
¼ teaspoon pepper
½ pound chicken (white or dark pieces)
1 cup precooked rice

Dissolve bouillon cube in hot water. Combine with all other ingredients except chicken and rice to make BBQ sauce. Place chicken in oven pan and pour sauce over chicken. Bake 45 minutes in a medium oven. Add precooked rice to pan 10 minutes before removing pan from oven.

UNCLE BEN'S CHICKEN

1 cup seasoned bread stuffing
½ cup water
2 boneless, skinless chicken breasts
1 cup precooked long-grain and wild-rice mixture
1 medium red pepper, cut in strips
1 medium green pepper, cut in strips
1 medium carrot, cut in strips

Mix stuffing and water. Flatten chicken breasts slightly (place between wax paper or foil and press with flat side of a knife) and spoon about half the stuffing onto breasts. Roll and secure with toothpick. Place chicken rolls in oven pan. Surround with precooked rice mixture. Arrange pepper and carrot strips on top. Cover with foil and bake 35 to 45 minutes in medium oven.

◑◑ GREAT FLAVORED BIRD

1 fresh lemon
1 tablespoon dried mustard
2 teaspoons brown sugar
½ teaspoon pepper
½ teaspoon coriander
2 boneless, skinless chicken breasts
nonstick cooking spray
¾ cup raisins
1 cup precooked noodles

Squeeze lemon and grate about 1 tablespoon of lemon zest (that's the outside of the peel). Combine juice, zest, and seasonings. Spray oven pan and place chicken in pan. Bake chicken for 15 minutes in medium to high oven (375°F, or lower rack setting in oven). Brush with sauce mixture, turn in pan, and bake another 15 minutes. Add raisins and remaining sauce. Bake 15 minutes. Serve with precooked noodles.

The next recipe calls for boneless chicken breasts with the skin still on. Most prepackaged boneless chicken breasts are also skinless, so you can't just run to the local supermarket and buy them. If you aren't lucky enough to have a butcher available to bone your chicken, buy regular chicken breasts and bone them yourself.

Start by turning the meat bone-side up. Assuming that the piece has part of the breast bone still attached, separate the meat from the edge of the bone with a small paring or boning knife. Turn the piece over and slide the blade between the ribs and the meat, cutting the meat away from the breast bone. You should, with practice, be able to bone a chicken breast without losing too much meat.

"PARDON ME, BUT DO YOU HAVE ANY . . . " CHICKEN

1 clove garlic, minced
2 tablespoons Dijon mustard
¼ teaspoon thyme
salt and pepper to taste
2 boneless chicken breasts (leave skin on)

Mix garlic with mustard, thyme, salt, and pepper. Lift up skin gently from meat and rub mixture on chicken. Replace skin and add some more salt and pepper. Place chicken in oven pan and bake 35 to 40 minutes on low rack. If you like, cut a potato in half, wrap it in foil, and bake it on the higher rack.

Up to this point, we've worked with basic variations on baked chicken. Now let's step up our creativity a notch.

UNUSUAL BIRD

  2 tablespoons Crisco shortening
  ⅓ cup flour
  salt and pepper to taste
  1½ cups milk
  2 eggs, beaten
  1 softpack chicken
  1 cup precooked rice
  ½ cup cheddar cheese (use reduced fat if you want), grated

In oven pan on stove, melt Crisco and stir in flour, salt, and pepper. Gradually add milk, stirring to keep from burning. Bring to boil. Remove from heat and add eggs. Stir with whisk until well blended. Stir in chicken. Cover with rice and then cheese. Bake in medium oven 20 minutes.

CRUMBY CHICKEN

  ½ cup seasoned breadcrumbs
  ¼ cup grated Parmesan cheese
  ¼ cup milk
  ½ pound chicken (white or dark pieces)
  1 medium yellow squash or zucchini, cut in 1-inch slices

Mix cheese and breadcrumbs. Dip chicken in milk and roll in coating mix. Place in oven pan. Dip squash in milk and then in coating mix. Arrange vegetables on top of chicken. Bake in medium oven 45 minutes.

BIG KING CHICKEN CASSEROLE

 2 tablespoons butter or margarine
 1 small green pepper, diced
 1 medium onion, diced
 4 or 5 medium mushrooms, sliced
 ¼ cup flour
 1 cup milk
 2 eggs, beaten
 1 tablespoon bottled or fresh pimiento pepper, thinly
   sliced
 pepper to taste
 1 softpack chicken
 breadcrumbs

In oven pan over medium flame, melt butter. Sauté green pepper, onion, and mushrooms. Add flour and blend. Add milk, eggs, pimiento, and pepper. Cook until thick, stirring constantly. Add chicken. Stir and remove from heat. Cover with layer of breadcrumbs and bake 25 minutes or until crust is brown.

POULET PIE

 1 packet powdered chicken gravy mix and 1 cup water
   to prepare
 2 prepared pie crusts
 1 softpack chicken
 2 medium carrots, diced
 1 large potato, thinly sliced
 2 stalks celery, diced

Prepare gravy mix in a metal cup over a medium to low flame. Line oven pan with one pie crust. Mix chicken, vegetables, and gravy and put in pan. Cover with other crust, pinching edges to seal. Cut slits in top crust to vent. Bake in medium oven 45 minutes or until pie crust is nicely browned.

CHEESY CHICKEN

   ½ cup milk (fresh, or from powdered)
   ½ cup Monterey Jack cheese (use reduced fat if you
      want), grated
   1 softpack chicken
   1 cup precooked macaroni
   1 medium red pepper, diced
   seasoned breadcrumbs

Over medium flame, heat milk to almost boiling in oven pan. Slowly add cheese and stir until smooth. Mix in chicken, macaroni, and red pepper. Sprinkle with breadcrumbs. Bake in a medium oven 25 minutes.

◖◗ HULA BIRD

   2 boneless, skinless chicken breasts
   ⅓ cup freeze-dried green beans, rehydrated
   1 orange, peeled and segmented
   1 8-ounce can crushed pineapple
   ½ teaspoon ginger
   ½ teaspoon cinnamon
   1 cup precooked rice

Place chicken breasts in oven pan. Surround with beans. Place orange segments over top and pour pineapple (including juice) over all. Sprinkle with cinnamon and ginger. Cover with foil (not needed with Outback Oven). Bake 45 minutes in medium to high oven (keep on upper rack, but use higher flame). If there's room in pan, add rice 5 minutes before serving. If not, remove chicken from oven at proper time. Wrap rice in foil and cook on top rack for 5 minutes.

◑◑ DIVINE CHICKEN

2 boneless, skinless chicken breasts
1½ cups broccoli florets
1 packet mushroom soup mix, reconstituted (single-
    serving size)
breadcrumbs

Line oven pan with foil. Place chicken in pan and cover
with broccoli. Pour mushroom soup over all. Sprinkle with
breadcrumbs. Cover and bake in medium oven 35 to 40
minutes. To crisp top, uncover last 5 to 10 minutes.

Paella is the national dish of Spain. This tasty blend of
meat, rice, vegetables, and broth starts out on top of the
stove and finishes up in the oven (use an Outback Oven).
The chef at Café Ba Ba Reeba in Chicago showed me a
great Paella de Verduras (vegetable paella). The following
is a meat-enhanced version of that recipe. Use the dark
meat from a chicken or turkey because the white meat will
dry out during cooking. You can also use pork shoulder,
which is moister than a tenderloin cut.

SQUARE-MEAL PAELLA

3 tablespoons olive oil
½ pound boneless chicken thigh meat, diced
½ pound mixed fresh vegetables (beans, cauliflower,
    broccoli, summer squash, etc.), chopped
1 teaspoon paprika
1 teaspoon garlic, minced
3 ounces tomato juice (½ small can; drink the rest)
2 threads saffron
1 15-ounce can chicken broth
8 ounces uncooked Spanish rice (if you use arborio, rinse
    with cold water before cooking to remove some of
    the starch)

Heat oil in oven pan over high flame and brown meat,
stirring frequently. Add the vegetables and sauté until

tender. Stir in paprika, garlic, and tomato juice. Add saffron, broth, and rice. Stir and bring to boil. Pan will be full; carefully assemble all pieces to set up oven. Bring heat indicator to "e" on Bake scale—or higher—and cook for 17 to 18 minutes. Remove from oven and let rest 2 to 3 minutes to allow remaining liquids to absorb.

Vegetarian Delights

A lot of these recipes can be considered side dishes, snacks, or à la carte fare. But you can make a full meal out of each one if you take the time to think about the four food groups. You can cover a lot of grain with a kaiser roll and a considerable amount of dairy protein with ½ cup of cheese. So try making one or more of these a centerpiece in your one-pan feast!

The next recipe works best in the Outback Oven because its wide, flat design makes it easy to get the pizza out of the pan.

ΰ THE ONE-PAN PIZZA

1 package pizza dough mix
2 teaspoons olive oil
1 large tomato, chopped or sliced razor-thin
¼ cup mushrooms, sliced
salt to taste
½ teaspoon oregano
½ teaspoon minced fresh basil
½ cup mozzarella cheese (use reduced fat if you want), grated

Prepare dough according to package directions. Flatten dough into a 10-inch circle. Rub with olive oil. Place in bottom pan of your Outback Oven. Sprinkle dough with tomato and then add mushrooms. Sprinkle with salt and spices and top with the cheese. (If you want to placate a meat lover, add small chunks of precooked sausage or thinly sliced pepperoni before you put on the cheese.) Bake in very hot oven about 10 to 15 minutes.

ʊ JOHN BARLEY CAKE

½ cup Bisquick
¾ cup water
½ cup uncooked barley (if you want, presoak for ½ hour in ½ cup water and then drain)
1 medium onion, diced
1 medium zucchini, diced
½ tablespoon vegetable oil
¼ teaspoon salt (optional)
¼ teaspoon oregano

Mix Bisquick with water; stir to remove lumps. Combine with remaining ingredients (add ½ cup water if you did not presoak barley) in greased oven pan. Cook in medium oven 30 minutes or until water is absorbed and top is firm.

You can try this to add a special touch to your camp table. (This may not work in an Outback Oven. There just isn't enough headroom for a rising soufflé.)

A-MAIZE-ING SOUFFLÉ

1 tablespoon butter or margarine, softened
1 tablespoon flour
¾ cup fresh corn (or use rehydrated freeze-dried)
1 cup hot milk
1 teaspoon salt (optional)
pepper and paprika to taste
2 eggs, separated

Blend butter and flour with a fork. To this, add corn, milk, salt, pepper, and paprika. Beat egg yolks until light and add to mixture. Beat egg whites until stiff and fold into mixture. Pour into oven pan and cook in medium-hot oven about 1 hour.

From this delicate taste treat, you could go all-American—or at least all-Wisconsin.

MACARONI AND CHEESE MOM'S WAY

1 cup milk
1½ cups Monterey Jack cheese (use reduced fat if you
　want), grated
3 cups precookd macaroni
½ cup seasoned breadcrumbs

Over medium flame, heat the milk until it almost boils.
Gradually add ¾ cup cheese, stirring so it doesn't burn.
When sauce is ready, pour over macaroni in oven pan.
Sprinkle with remaining cheese and then with bread-crumbs. Cook in medium oven 25 to 30 minutes or until
breadcrumbs are toasty brown.

NO-NOODLE LASAGNA

1 medium eggplant, cut in ¼-inch slices (about 10 to 12
　slices)
salt to taste
1 or 2 eggs
½ cup milk
½ cup olive oil
½ cup seasoned breadcrumbs
2 cups spaghetti sauce
8 ounces provolone cheese (use reduced fat if you
　want), sliced

Sprinkle sliced eggplant with salt (if desired) and set
aside on towel to drain for 10 minutes. Then rinse. Beat
egg(s) with milk. Heat oil in pan over medium flame. Dip
eggplant in egg mixture and then into breadcrumbs (both
sides). Brown both sides in hot oil. Set on towel to drain.
Remove oil from pan and wipe clean. Alternate layers of
eggplant, sauce, and cheese in pan, repeating until ingre-dients are used up. Bake in medium oven 25 to 30 minutes.

♌ CHEESY SPUDS

4 medium potatoes, thinly sliced
6 ounces ham (optional), diced (use turkey ham if you
   want)
½ cup cheddar cheese (use reduced fat if you want),
   grated
1 large onion, thinly sliced
¾ cup milk
2 tablespoons flour
salt and pepper to taste

Place potatoes in oven pan and add layers of ham,
cheese, and onion. Whisk together milk, flour, salt, and
pepper. Pour over mixture in pan. Bake in medium oven
45 minutes. Sprinkle breadcrumbs on top if you wish.

♌ PEPPERS À LA SHROOM

2 medium green peppers
¾ cup mushrooms, sliced
1 medium tomato, chopped
½ cup mozzarella cheese (use reduced fat if you want),
   grated
½ teaspoon oregano
¼ teaspoon fennel seed
breadcrumbs

Cut tops off green peppers and clean out seeds. Combine mushrooms, tomato, cheese, oregano, and fennel.
Stuff peppers. (You can add ½ cup precooked rice to stuffing if desired.) Sprinkle breadcrumbs over the top and
cook in medium oven 30 to 45 minutes (control heat with
the flame because you might have to use the lower rack to
accommodate height of peppers).

Sticking with stuffed vegetables for a moment . . .

FULL-HOUSE MUSHROOMS

4 to 6 very large mushrooms
1 small onion, minced
¼ cup fresh spinach leaves, minced
2 teaspoons olive oil
½ teaspoon basil
¼ teaspoon salt (optional)
¼ teaspoon pepper
1 tablespoon grated Parmesan cheese
2 tablespoons breadcrumbs

Remove stems from mushrooms. Mince them and combine with remaining ingredients. If mixture doesn't stick together, add more breadcrumbs. Press stuffing firmly into each mushroom cap, mounding stuffing ½ inch or so above edge of cap. Place in oven pan and bake in hot oven (400°F) 10 minutes or until stuffing begins to brown. Serves 1, maybe 2.

ART-I-CHOKE ON THESE TOMATOES?

1 large tomato
2 marinated artichoke hearts
1 teaspoon olive oil
3 tablespoons seasoned breadcrumbs
2 thick slices provolone cheese (use reduced fat if you want)
2 jumbo green olives stuffed with pimento

Cut tomato in half. Out of each half, scoop a hole just large enough to hold an artichoke heart. Insert a heart into each tomato half. Mix oil with breadcrumbs and press a handful on top of each tomato half. Bake in medium oven 20 minutes. Lay slice of cheese on top and complete with olive on top of that. Bake another 5 minutes or until cheese melts (but does not run or burn). Serves 1.

Packed with protein, calcium, B vitamins, and fiber, this meal will keep you full for hours. The beans and rice provide protein complementation, and the cheese and cottage cheese supply additional protein.

CHEESY BEANS AND RICE

1½ cups precooked brown rice
½ can (7½ ounces) kidney beans, drained and repackaged
1 clove garlic, minced
1 medium onion, chopped
1 4-ounce can chopped green chili peppers
4 ounces jack cheese (use reduced fat if you want), grated
1 cup low-fat cottage cheese
½ cup (2 ounces) sharp cheddar cheese (use reduced fat if you want), grated

In bowl, combine rice, beans, garlic, onion, and chili peppers. Layer this mixture alternately with the jack cheese and the cottage cheese in an oiled pan. End with a layer of the bean-rice mixture. Bake in medium oven 30 minutes. During the last few minutes of baking, sprinkle the cheddar cheese on top.

Here's a great lunch recipe to serve hot or cold. I usually make it ahead of time and serve it cold with a fruit salad. This recipe is very high in protein, iron, calcium, vitamin A, and beta-carotene. It is also relatively low in fat since there is no pie crust. If you don't like spinach, you can substitute broccoli.

CRUSTLESS SPINACH PIE

> 1 10-ounce package frozen chopped spinach or broccoli, thawed and well drained (or use fresh spinach or broccoli, cooked, well drained, and chopped)
> ½ pound sharp cheddar or feta cheese (use reduced fat if you want), grated or crumbled
> 2 cups low-fat cottage cheese
> 4 eggs
> 6 tablespoons flour
> ¼ teaspoon salt
> ½ teaspoon pepper

In a bowl, combine spinach, grated cheese, and cottage cheese. In a cup, mix eggs with a fork and add flour, salt, and pepper. Combine both mixtures and mix well. Place mixture in a lightly oiled or nonstick-sprayed pie pan, and bake 1 hour in medium oven.

Of course, you can also use your oven simply to bake vegetables.

☉ SOLID SQUASH SURPRISE

> 1 small acorn squash (1 to 1½ pounds)
> 1 orange, peeled and halved
> 2 tablespoons brown sugar
> 2 tablespoons butter of margarine

Cut squash in half along the equator. Clean out seeds. Trim ends so that the halves do not roll onto their sides. Push half of orange into each cavity, enlarging the cavity as needed. Divide sugar and butter evenly and place on top of orange. Cover with foil. Place in pan and bake in hot oven 40 minutes or until squash is tender.

Beef

Here's where the trail oven can make a big difference in a trekker's life. The land of roasts, of exciting combinations of richly flavored meats and interesting sauces, will come to life as you light up your life and your oven.

The variety of cuts available to the outdoor chef make beef a versatile choice. Whether you decide to use hamburger or steak, there's always something fun to cook. Remember, though, that beef can be fatty, gristly, tough, or a combination thereof. Cooks, both famous and mundane, have found ways to turn inexpensive beef into toothsome meals fit for lord and lady.

◐◐ SHEPHERD'S PIE

3 large potatoes, peeled and thinly sliced
water
salt
3 tablespoons "lite" margarine
½ cup milk (fresh, or from powdered)
¾ pound ground beef (use 95 percent lean)
salt and pepper to taste
¼ cup flour
¼ cup water
2 to 3 carrots, chopped
1 stalk celery, chopped
1 large onion, chopped

Using your oven pan as a pot, place potatoes in salted water and boil 15 minutes. Drain water. Mash potatoes with butter and milk. Remove from pan and set aside. Clean pan. Over medium flame, brown hamburger until crumbly. Reduce heat and add salt, pepper, flour, and water. Stir to make gravy. Remove from heat. Add vegetables and stir to mix. Make crust of mashed potatoes over the top of the meat-and-vegetable mixture. Bake 35 minutes in medium oven.

Tip: If you want, substitute 2 cups instant mashed potatoes, prepared according to package directions, for the potatoes, butter, and milk.

A DIFFERENT SORT OF ONION

1 large onion, halved, centers removed (reserve for sauce)
¼ pound each ground beef and ground pork
¼ cup salted peanuts, chopped or crushed
¼ teaspoon pepper
⅛ teaspoon nutmeg
1 beef bouillon cube
1 cup boiling water
1 15-ounce can whole tomatoes, drained, chopped, and divided in half

Sauce
onion centers
½ divided tomatoes
¼ cup mushrooms, chopped
2 tablespoons sour cream
2 tablespoons Madeira wine

Cut onion in half and remove center (save), leaving two "cups." Mix beef, pork, nuts, pepper, and nutmeg. Stuff onion halves. Place in oven pan. Dissolve bouillon cube in water, add half of tomatoes, and pour into pan. Bake in medium oven 1 hour. While main dish is cooking, make sauce. Mince onion centers and combine with mushrooms, remaining tomatoes, sour cream, and wine. Heat on stove in small pan. Pour sauce over onion halves before serving.

‹› DEEP-DISH STEAK

¾ pound round steak, 1½ inches thick
¼ cup flour
1 teaspoon salt (optional)
¼ teaspoon pepper
nonstick cooking spray
1 medium onion, chopped
1 medium green pepper, chopped
1 stalk celery, chopped
⅓ cup raisins
2 large tomatoes, cut in chunks

Mix flour, salt, and pepper. Rub into steak. Spray oven
pan and heat over medium flame. Brown meat on both
sides. Remove from heat. Add remaining ingredients.
Cover and bake in medium oven 1 to 1½ hours. Turn meat
occasionally. Serve with bread.

DON CARLOS'S STEAK SURPRISE

1 tablespoon olive oil
3 green onions, chopped
1 medium green pepper, sliced
1 large tomato, chopped
1 clove garlic, minced
¾ pound top round steak, cut in thin strips
1 teaspoon chili powder
½ teaspoon salt (optional)

In oven pan over medium flame, sauté vegetables in oil
until tender. Add meat and brown briefly. Remove from
heat. Add seasonings and stir until well coated. Cover and
bake in medium oven 35 to 40 minutes.

MERRY-NADE POT ROAST

¾ pound chuck steak or small rump or round roast
¼ cup Italian salad dressing
3 tablespoons butter, margarine, or vegetable oil
½ cup water
1 large onion, sliced
3 carrots, sliced
2 large potatoes, cut in chunks
2 tablespoons water
1 teaspoon flour

Pour salad dressing over meat. In oven pan over medium flame, melt 2 tablespoons butter, add meat, and brown. Remove from heat and add ½ cup water and vegetables. Bake in medium oven 1 hour. Remove meat from pan, place pan on stove over medium flame, and add remaining tablespoon butter. Whisk flour and 2 tablespoons water together and stir into sauce to thicken gravy.

Staying Italian for a moment . . .

ʘ KATIE'S LASAGNA

¾ pound ground beef (use 95 percent lean)
1½ to 2 cups spaghetti sauce
1 cup ricotta cheese (use reduced fat if you want)
½ cup grated Parmesan cheese (freshly grated is best)
8 ounces precooked lasagna noodles (or use "oven-ready" noodles)

Brown beef in baking pan over medium flame. Drain and add spaghetti sauce. Remove meat-sauce mixture from pan to bowl. Do not clean pan. Combine cheeses in bowl. Place single layer of noodles on bottom of pan. Top noodles with layer of cheese, followed by layer of sauce. Repeat until you run out of noodles. (You might have to cut noodles in half to accommodate reduced pan size.) Bake uncovered in medium oven 35 to 40 minutes.

☼ SAUCY BEEF

¾ pound top or bottom round, cut in bite-size chunks
¼ cup flour
salt and pepper to taste
2 tablespoons prepared mustard
2 teaspoons vegetable oil
1 large onion, diced
1 beef bouillon cube
1 cup boiling water
2 large potatoes, thinly sliced
½ cup sour cream (use nonfat if you want)

Rub flour on meat. Season with salt and pepper. Rub mustard on meat. Heat oil in oven pan and brown meat. Add onion and sauté until tender. Remove from heat. Dissolve bouillon cube in water and pour over meat. Add potatoes. Bake in medium oven 45 minutes. Just before serving, stir in sour cream—this creates an incredible sauce. Serve with fresh carrot sticks and rolls.

☼ RED-EYE STEW

¾ pound stew beef, cut in 1-inch cubes
1 tablespoon vegetable oil
1 large onion, chopped
½ teaspoon salt (optional)
1 teaspoon paprika
¼ teaspoon caraway seeds
1 6-ounce can tomato paste
1 beef bouillon cube dissolved in 1 cup hot water
2 large potatoes, peeled and cut in 1-inch cubes

In oven pan, heat oil over medium flame and brown beef. Reduce heat and sauté onion. Remove from heat and add all ingredients except potatoes. Cover and bake 1 hour in medium oven. Stir in potatoes and cook another 35 minutes. Serve with hard rolls.

BIG BEN BEEF BAKE

¼ cup honey
¼ cup BBQ sauce
1 tablespoon vegetable oil
2 tablespoons lemon juice
¾ pound flank steak
1 large onion, cut in chunks
1 medium red pepper, sliced

Combine honey, BBQ sauce, oil, and lemon juice to make a sauce. Rub into meat and let it rest in sauce 10 to 15 minutes. Place meat in oven pan and surround with vegetables. Pour any remaining sauce over all. Bake 15 to 20 minutes in medium to hot oven. Serve with precooked and reheated noodles.

BBQ BRISKET

¾ to 1 pound beef brisket
1 cup BBQ sauce
1 large onion, sliced

Rub sauce into meat and let stand 30 minutes. Place in oven pan with onion and sauce. Cover and bake in low to medium oven for 1 to 1½ hours. Slice across grain and serve on hard roll or with rice, accompanied by fresh fruit and some vegetables.

Stepping up your meat selection a notch can bring even more interesting taste variations. By purchasing sirloin, eye of round, and filet, you'll be putting four-star restaurant quality on your outdoor table. You can reduce the fat count by choosing Select cuts. "Select" is a USDA grade that means those cuts have less marbling than "Choice" or "Prime." However, with many oven dishes you may have a better outcome with the fattier pieces as they are less likely to dry out during cooking.

CAP O' FILET (IT'S THE TOP!)

2 filets mignons (each about 4 to 6 ounces and 1½ inches thick)
2 tablespoons liver pâté
1 tablespoon plus 1 teaspoon olive oil
1 teaspoon celery salt (optional)
¼ cup Gruyère cheese (use reduced fat if you want), grated
2 tablespoons minced fresh spinach
2 tablespoons seasoned breadcrumbs
2 large mushrooms
2 slices Gruyère cheese (use reduced fat if you want) (¼ inch thick)

Make a pocket in each filet by cutting into side; be careful not to cut filets in half. Stuff each cavity with 1 tablespoon pâté (it should not squirt out past edge). Rub 1 tablespoon oil on meat and season with celery salt. Set aside. Mix grated cheese, spinach, breadcrumbs, and 1 teaspoon oil. Remove stems of mushrooms. Carefully cut off part of each cap to make flat surface. Stuff mushrooms with cheese mixture. Place meat in oven pan and bake in medium oven about 20 minutes. Place a slice of cheese and a mushroom on top of each filet and continue baking another 10 minutes.

RIB-EYE ECSTASY

½ teaspoon each salt (optional) and pepper
1 teaspoon paprika
½ teaspoon garlic powder
1 tablespoon corn oil
2 rib-eye steaks, about ½ pound each
1 large onion, sliced
1 cup rehydrated corn

Combine seasonings. Rub both sides of steaks with oil and seasonings. Lay onion on bottom of oven pan and place meat on top. Cover and bake in hot oven 20 minutes. After first 15 minutes, spoon corn onto meat. You can add a little steak sauce after cooking, if you like.

〇〇 BARON BEEF

1 pound eye-of-round roast
1 tablespoon Kitchen Bouquet Browning and Seasoning
    Sauce
1 teaspoon each salt (optional), pepper, and thyme

Rub Kitchen Bouquet over meat. Mix salt, pepper, and thyme and rub on meat. Place roast in oven pan. Bake 15 minutes in very hot oven. Reduce heat and continue baking for another hour.

Tip: To complete your meal, wrap some thickly sliced carrots, green onions, and red and green peppers in foil (season with a dash of sesame oil) and add to oven for the last 30 minutes of baking. You could also bake a potato (cut in half and wrapped in foil).

Pork, Ham, and Other "Ovenables"

Ovens make a big difference in the way you eat when trekking. Take pork, for example. Sure, you can fry a chop or dice up some loin and mix it with veggies. But imagine the lip smacking that will ensue when you fire up the oven and make a mess of ribs or a roast smothered in applesauce. (Remember to cook your pork thoroughly!) Think about how good your stomach will feel when you wrap yourself around a mouth-watering casserole that highlights ham and cheese. Enough thinking. How about some eating?

CORTLAND PORK ROAST

¾ pound boneless pork loin roast
1 tablespoon vegetable oil
3 tablespoons brown sugar
1 medium apple, chopped
½ cup applesauce
1 teaspoon cinnamon
1 teaspoon nutmeg

Rub oil and then 1 tablespoon brown sugar onto roast. Bake in a medium oven 45 minutes. Combine apple, applesauce, 2 tablespoons brown sugar, and spices. Spoon over roast. Cover and bake another 45 minutes. Serve with reheated rice and relish tray of pickles, olives, pickled beets, and celery.

◑ CHAMPIGNON CHOPS

2 center-cut boneless pork loin chops
1 packet mushroom soup (single-serving size) and water
    to prepare
parsley, chopped
1 large potato, sliced

In oven pan, brown chops in a little oil. Remove from heat and pour mushroom soup over top. Sprinkle with parsley. Lay potato slices around edge of pan. Cover and bake 45 minutes in medium oven.

◑ "NOT THE COLD SHOULDER" PORK ROAST

1 to 1½ pound pork shoulder roast, well trimmed of all
    visible fat
1 tablespoon (or more) caraway seeds
salt and pepper to taste
1 15-ounce can sauerkraut, drained

Rub spices onto meat. Spread sauerkraut evenly across the bottom of the pan. Place roast on top, cover with foil, and bake in medium oven for 1½ hours. Serve with spiced apple slices. Serves 3 or 4.

ʊʊ MOM'S TUNA-NOODLE CASSEROLE

nonstick cooking spray
2 cups precooked egg noodles
1 6-ounce can solid-white tuna, drained (or softpack)
1 packet mushroom soup mix (single-serving size) and
    ¾ of the water suggested to prepare
¼ cup parsley, chopped
1 tablespoon butter or margarine (use "lite" margarine
    if you want), melted
breadcrumbs

In lightly sprayed oven pan, mix noodles, tuna, soup, and parsley. Drizzle melted butter on top. Sprinkle breadcrumbs over all. Bake 35 minutes in medium oven.

LANAI GROUND LOIN

nonstick cooking spray
¾ pound ground pork tenderloin
½ teaspoon salt (optional)
1 medium Vidalia (sweet) onion, diced
1 medium red pepper, diced
¼ teaspoon dry mustard
2 eggs, beaten
¾ cup breadcrumbs
½ cup crushed pineapple

Spray oven pan. Combine all ingredients in pan and bake in medium oven 45 minutes. Serve hot with freshly sliced uncooked summer squash or zucchini.

ITALIAN SAUSAGE BAKE-OFF

¾ pound mild Italian sausage
1 15-ounce can tomato sauce
½ teaspoon oregano
½ teaspoon basil
½ teaspoon garlic powder
1 bay leaf
¼ teaspoon fennel seed
2 teaspoons sugar
2 teaspoons grated Parmesan cheese
1 large onion, chopped
1 large green pepper, sliced
1 zucchini, sliced
1 large tomato, diced
6 slices provolone cheese (use reduced fat if you want)

In oven pan, brown sausage over medium heat. In bowl, mix tomato sauce, seasonings, sugar, and Parmesan to make marinara sauce. Remove pan from heat, drain grease, and mix in vegetables. Pour sauce over all. Lay slices of provolone cheese over top and bake in hot oven 35 to 40 minutes. Serve over precooked pasta.

Here's an easy meal that will fill you up.

BIG BBQ RIBS

4 farmer-style (with meat on, not spareribs) pork ribs
¾ cup BBQ sauce
1 large onion, cut in chunks
1½ cups precooked rice

In oven pan, place ribs and smother with BBQ sauce. Pack onion around ribs. Bake in medium oven 45 minutes to 1 hour. About 10 minutes before ribs are done, add rice right on top of the ribs.

YAM 'N' HAM

1 pound smoked shoulder or canned ham
whole cloves
⅓ cup brown sugar
2 medium sweet potatoes, quartered
2 tablespoons butter or margarine

Place meat in oven pan. Stud ham with cloves and sprinkle with brown sugar. Place sweet potatoes around meat, skin side down, and dab with butter. Cover and bake in medium oven 75 minutes. Serve with reheated rice or prepare a packaged red beans and rice dish.

PORK PIE (NOT THE HAT)

1 package prepared pie crust (2 crusts)
¼ cup bacon bits
2 large potatoes, thinly sliced
1 large onion, diced
salt and pepper to taste
1 teaspoon sage
2 cups precooked pork loin, diced
1 packet brown gravy mix and 1 cup water to prepare

Line oven pan with one pie crust. Sprinkle with bacon bits. Layer potatoes and onion. Mix salt, pepper, sage, and pork and make a final layer. Pour gravy over all. Cover with second pie crust. Pinch edges and cut a few vents in top. Bake in medium oven 1 hour.

SMOKEHOUSE SPECIAL

½ cup milk
½ cup cheddar cheese (use reduced fat if you want),
    grated
2 tablespoons flour
1 cup ham, diced
2 medium potatoes, peeled and thinly sliced
1 medium onion, sliced
2 to 3 tablespoons breadcrumbs

In oven pan, heat milk to near boiling. Gradually add cheese and flour to make sauce, whisking to avoid lumps. Remove from heat and stir in ham, potatoes, and onion. Stir to mix well. Sprinkle breadcrumbs over the top and bake in medium oven 45 minutes.

Baked Goods

With an oven in hand, you can make bread, rolls, and biscuits. You can also bake cakes and pies, but look for those in the Dessert section, beginning on page 164.

A lot of the prepackaged rolls you can buy will keep a day or two without overt refrigeration. Simply pack the cylinder near your frozen meat to keep it cool until you're ready to bake them. Then follow package instructions.

If you're a bit more ambitious, you can start from scratch. There's been a lot written about in-camp breads, so I'll include only my favorites here.

BIG D'S BISCUITS

1 cup flour
1 teaspoon baking powder
pinch of salt (optional)
2 teaspoons vegetable oil
½ cup water

Combine all ingredients, adding just enough water to make a good stiff dough. Flour your hands and form biscuits about 2 inches in diameter and 1 inch thick. Place on greased oven pan. Bake 10 to 15 minutes in a medium oven, checking to see that biscuits don't burn.

HI-HO CORNBREAD

1½ cups flour
⅔ cup yellow cornmeal
4 tablespoons sugar
salt (optional)
2 teaspoons baking powder
2 eggs, beaten
1 cup milk
4 tablespoons vegetable oil

Mix dry ingredients. Add wet ingredients, stirring to mix batter evenly. Pour batter in greased oven pan and bake 25 minutes in a hot oven. Check with straw or toothpick for doneness, and make sure bread doesn't burn.

CONFETTI CORNBREAD

To Hi-Ho Cornbread recipe, add ¼ cup diced red pepper, ¼ cup diced green pepper, and 1 teaspoon minced fresh cilantro. You can also stir in ¼ cup of grated cheddar cheese. Add 10 to 15 minutes to cooking time to account for additional moisture from veggies.

This next recipe works great in a frying pan, too. Simply cook the patties 2 to 3 minutes per side or until browned.

HUSH MY PUPPIES

 1 cup yellow cornmeal
 ½ teaspoon salt (optional)
 ½ teaspoon baking powder
 1 egg, beaten
 ½ cup milk
 1 tablespoon minced onion
 1 tablespoon vegetable oil

Combine dry ingredients. Add egg, milk, and onion. Mix together to form dough. Shape into ½-inch oblong patties and place on greased oven pan. Brush tops with oil and bake in hot oven 10 to 15 minutes or until nicely browned.

SHORTCAKE BISCUITS

 1 cup flour
 1½ teaspoons baking powder
 1½ tablespoons sugar
 ¼ teaspoon salt (optional)
 1 egg, beaten
 ⅓ cup milk
 2 tablespoons vegetable oil

Combine all ingredients and mix. Dough should be stiff. If it seems too loose, add flour as needed. Coat hands with flour and form biscuits about ½ to ¾ inch thick and 3 inches across. Bake in hot oven 15 minutes.

PAM'S SPECIAL "THINGS"

2 cups Bisquick mix
⅔ cup milk
1 tablespoon flour
3 to 4 tablespoons brown sugar
1 to 2 tablespoons cinnamon
½ cup chopped nuts
½ cup raisins
2 tablespoons butter
shortening or oil

In mixing bowl combine Bisquick and milk. Cut a 12-by-18-inch piece of wax paper. Place on cutting mat or board and sprinkle lightly with flour. Place dough on wax paper and roll or press dough into an 8-by-14-inch rectangle, about ¼ inch thick. Spread 3 tablespoons of brown sugar evenly on the dough, then sprinkle with 1 tablespoon of cinnamon, and nuts and raisins. Put small bits of butter on top. Roll up the dough lengthwise. Use the wax paper to lift dough and help roll. Cut the roll into ½- to ¾-inch slices. Arrange slices on greased cookie sheet. Put pan in medium (350°F) oven. Cook for 15 to 20 minutes until browned with a crisp sugary crust on top.

DESSERT

Do you like dessert? The oven is the way to go for after-dinner tasties. Any cake mix will do for starters, and brownies fill you up after a long day of trekking. And all of those come in prepackaged, ready-to-go form. Just visit the baking aisle at your store. And, if you're daring, you can build your dessert from scratch.

Remember that you have to watch the oven temperature or else you might end up with a charred "might have been." Test for doneness by sticking a toothpick into the middle of the cake. If it comes out clean, the cake is done.

The following recipes work well outdoors, both when you're cooking and when you're eating.

◑◑ POWERFUL GINGERBREAD

¼ cup butter or margarine
¼ cup sugar
1 egg, beaten
1 cup flour
½ teaspoon baking soda
½ teaspoon cinnamon
½ teaspoon ginger
¼ teaspoon ground cloves
¼ teaspoon salt (optional)
⅓ cup molasses
½ cup hot water
¼ cup raisins
nonstick cooking spray

Cream butter and sugar in a bowl with a fork. Mix in egg. Combine dry ingredients in a cup or bowl. Mix molasses and hot water in a cup. Alternate adding dry ingredients and molasses mixture to sugar and egg. Beat until smooth. Stir in raisins. Spray baking pan and pour in batter. Bake in medium oven for about 45 minutes.

☺ APPLE HEAVEN

2 medium apples (McIntosh are best), thinly sliced
2 tablespoons brown sugar
½ teaspoon cinnamon
½ teaspoon nutmeg
2 teaspoons butter or margarine

Place apples in oven pan. Sprinkle with brown sugar and spices and place dots of butter all around. Cover and bake in medium oven 20 minutes.

APPLE-CINNAMON COFFEE CAKE

½ cup applesauce
¼ cup brown sugar
2 teaspoons cinnamon
¼ cup milk
1 egg, beaten
1½ cups Bisquick

Topping
½ cup brown sugar
2 tablespoons butter or margarine

To make cake, lightly mix applesauce, brown sugar, cinnamon, milk, and egg. Gradually add Bisquick until you have a smooth batter. Pour into greased oven pan. To make topping, use a fork to cream ingredients together until crumbly. Sprinkle over top of batter. Bake in medium oven 25 minutes or until center of coffee cake is done.

☮ BLUE-TOOTH COBBLER

½ cup blueberries (substitute apples, thinly sliced, if
    desired)
½ teaspoon cinnamon
¼ teaspoon nutmeg
½ teaspoon flour
1 cup Bisquick
2 tablespoons butter or margarine
¼ cup sugar
1 egg, beaten
½ cup milk

In greased oven pan, combine blueberries, spices, and
flour. In bowl, mix all other ingredients and pour over
fruit mixture. Bake in medium oven 25 minutes or until
top is browned. Turn out upside down onto serving plate.

OOPS, I FLIPPED THE PINEAPPLE CAKE UPSIDE DOWN!

2 tablespoons vegetable oil
⅓ cup brown sugar
1 8-ounce can sliced pineapple, drained
1 9-ounce box Jiffy yellow cake mix
1 egg, beaten (substitute 2 tablespoons whole egg pow-
    der, if desired)
½ cup water (if you use egg powder, add 3 tablespoons
    water)

In oven pan, swirl oil until bottom of pan is covered.
Press brown sugar into oil, creating an even layer that cov-
ers only the bottom of the pan. Lay pineapple on the
sugar. Set aside. In bowl, mix the dry cake mix and egg
until fully blended. Add water and beat for 3 to 4 minutes.
Pour evenly over fruit and sugar. Set Outback Oven on top
of stove. Heat over medium to high flame until temperature indicator reaches Bake. Cook for 25 minutes, adjust-
ing flame as needed.

TWOTI-FRUITI PIE

1 package prepared pie crust (2 crusts)
½ cup blueberries
¾ cup apples, thinly sliced
¼ cup sugar
½ teaspoon cinnamon
¼ teaspoon nutmeg
1 teaspoon flour
1 tablespoon butter or margarine

Place one pie crust in bottom of oven pan. In bowl, mix all other ingredients except butter. Pour onto crust. Dot top of filling with butter and cover with top crust. Pinch edges and cut vents in top. Sprinkle top crust with a few drops of water. Bake in medium oven 45 minutes

Tip: Use this recipe to make apple pie; just omit the blueberries and double the amount of apples.

APPENDIX

Menu Planning

When you plan your trail menu, the first step is to decide whether you feel like eating pan, pot, or oven food, or—if you've got companions to share the cookware load—some combination thereof. I offered a pan menu in The Food chapter. Here are two more possible menus, one for a pot and one for an oven, and associated shopping lists for a modest weekend outing—reaching the trailhead after dinner Friday and heading home after Sunday breakfast. Build from there for longer trips.

POT

Saturday Breakfast
Eggs à la Goldenrod (page 90)

Saturday Lunch
Fast Pea Soup (see page 103)

Saturday Dinner
Pedro's Rice (see page 116)
Indian Pudding (see page 125)

Snacks
oranges

Sunday Breakfast
Soy Sauce Steak Sunrise (see page 88)
hard-boiled eggs

SHOPPING LIST

Provisions (staples)
coffee
juice mix
milk (powdered)
hot chocolate mix
wine
flour
nonstick cooking
    spray
salt
pepper (black and
    white)
sugar (white,
    brown, sugar
    subst.)

Carbs
bread (4 slices)
rice (¾ cup
    uncooked)
cornmeal (¾ cup)
crackers

Proteins
eggs (6+)
ham (½ cup diced)
ground beef (½ lb.)
sirloin (½ lb.)

Vegetables/Fruits
oranges
tomatoes (5 plum)
raisins (¼ cup)
peas (1 cup freeze-
    dried)
onion (1)
green pepper (1)
carrots (2)

Fats/Oils
butter or
margarine
    (3 tbsp.)

Sweeteners/Spices
thyme (1 tsp.)
chili powder
    (½ tsp.)
nutmeg (½ tsp.)
cinnamon (½ tsp.)
soy sauce (⅓ cup)
honey (2 tbsp.)
sweetened con-
    densed milk
    (1 can)

OVEN

Saturday Breakfast

Amsterdam Apple Pancake (see pages 132–33)

Saturday Lunch

beef stick
cheese
bread
carrots

(continued)

Saturday Dinner

Cheesy Spuds (see page 144)
Blue-Tooth Cobbler (see page 166)

Snacks

cashews and raisins

Sunday Breakfast

Bermuda Eggs (see page 132)

SHOPPING LIST

Provisions (staples)

coffee
juice mix
milk (powdered)
hot chocolate mix
wine
flour
nonstick cooking
  spray
salt
pepper (black
  and white)
sugar (white,
  brown, sugar
  subst.)

Carbs

bread
Bisquick (1⅔ cup)
potatoes (4)
breadcrumbs
  (2 tbsp.)

Proteins

eggs (5)
beef stick (⅓ lb.)
ham (6 oz.)
cheese (½ cup
    cheddar, 1 tbsp.
    Parmesan, ½ lb.
    other)

Vegetables/Fruits

apples (2)
blueberries
  (½ cup)
raisins
carrots
parsley (2 tbsp.)
onions (1 yellow,
  1 Bermuda)

Fats/Oils

cashews
butter or marga-
  rine (4 tbsp.)

Sweeteners/Spices

nutmeg (¼ tsp.)
tarragon (¼ tsp.)
cinnamon (1 tsp.)

SAMPLE MENU FORM

DAY 1_____   **Page #**

Dinner

_____   _____
_____   _____
_____   _____

DAY 2_____

Breakfast

_____   _____
_____   _____

Lunch

_____   _____
_____   _____

Dinner

_____   _____
_____   _____
_____   _____

DAY 3_____

Breakfast

_____   _____
_____   _____

Weights and Measures

Weight
1 ounce = 28.35 grams
1 pound = 16 ounces = 453.6 grams
2.2 pounds = 1 kilogram

Volume
1 teaspoon = 5 milliliters
1 tablespoon = 3 teaspoons = 15 milliliters
1 fluid ounce = 6 teaspoons = ⅛ cup = 29.56 milliliters
1 cup = 16 tablespoons = 8 fluid ounces = 236 milliliters
1 pint = 16 fluid ounces = 2 cups = 0.5 liter
1 quart = 32 fluid ounces = 2 pints = 0.9 liter
1 gallon = 128 fluid ounces = 4 quarts = 3.8 liters

Length
1 inch = 2.54 centimeters

Thermometer
To convert:
(°F − 32) x 0.555 = °C
(°C x 1.8) + 32 = °F

slow oven = 300°–325°F (150°–165°C)
medium oven = 350°–375°F (175°–185°C)
hot oven = 400°–425°F (205°–220°C)

NUTRITIONAL CONTENT OF SOME COMMON FOODS

Food	Kilocalories per 3½ Ounces	% Fat	% Protein	% Carbohydrate
Dairy products, fats, and oils				
margarine	720	81.0	0.6	0.4
low-fat spread	366	36.8	6.0	3.0
vegetable oil	900	100.0	—	—
instant dried skim milk	355	1.3	36.0	53.0
cheddar cheese	398	32.2	25.0	2.1
Edam cheese	305	23.0	24.0	—
Parmesan cheese	410	30.0	35.0	—
eggs, dried	592	41.2	47.0	4.1
low-fat cheese spread	175	9.0	20.0	4.0
Dried fruit				
apples	275	—	1.0	78.0
apricots	261	—	5.0	66.5
dates	275	—	2.2	72.9
figs	275	—	4.3	69.1
peaches	261	—	3.1	68.3
raisins	289	—	2.5	77.4
Vegetables				
potatoes, dehydrated	352	—	8.3	80.4
tomato flakes	342	—	10.8	76.7
baked beans	123	2.6	6.1	19.0
Nuts				
almonds	600	57.7	18.6	19.5
Brazil nuts	652	66.9	14.3	10.9
coconut, desiccated	605	62.0	6.0	6.0
peanut butter	589	49.4	27.8	17.2
peanuts, roasted	582	49.8	26.0	18.8
Grains				
oatmeal	375	7.0	11.0	62.4
muesli, sweetened	348	6.3	10.4	66.6
pasta, white	370	—	12.5	75.2
pasta, whole wheat	323	0.5	12.5	67.2
rice, brown	359	—	7.5	77.4
rice, white	363	—	6.7	80.4
flour, plain	360	2.0	11.0	75.0
flour, wholemeal	345	3.0	12.0	72.0

(continued)

NUTRITIONAL CONTENT OF SOME COMMON FOODS *(continued)*

Food	Kilocalories per 3½ Ounces	% Fat	% Protein	% Carbo- hydrate
Baked products				
granola bar	382	13.4	4.9	64.4
crispbread, rye	345	1.2	13.0	76.3
oat crackers	369	15.7	10.1	65.6
bread, white	271	—	8.7	50.5
bread, wholemeal	243	—	10.5	47.7
cookies, chocolate	525	28.0	6.0	67.0
fig bar	356	5.6	3.9	75.4
cake, fruit	355	13.0	5.0	58.0
Meat and fish				
beef, dried	204	6.3	34.3	—
beef, corned, canned	264	18.0	23.5	—
salami	490	45.0	19.0	2.0
salmon, canned	151	7.1	20.8	—
sardines, drained	165	11.1	24.0	—
tuna, drained	165	8.2	28.8	—
Sugars and sweets				
honey	303	—	0.3	82.0
sugar, brown	373	—	—	96.4
sugar, white	384	—	—	99.5
chocolate, milk	518	32.3	7.7	56.9
custard, instant	378	10.2	2.9	72.6
Drinks				
cocoa (mix)	391	10.6	9.4	73.9
coffee	2	—	0.2	—
tea	1	—	0.1	—

Adapted from *Agricultural Handbook No. 8: Composition of Foods* (U.S. Department of Agriculture); *Food Facts* by David Briggs and Mark Wahlqvist; and manufacturer's specifications. Courtesy of *The Backpacker's Handbook* by Chris Townsend (Ragged Mountain Press, 2005).

INDEX